MY EXPERIENCES IN
WORLD WAR II

MY EXPERIENCES IN
WORLD WAR II

OBSERVATIONS AND INSIGHTS OF A NAVAL INTELLIGENCE OFFICER

ELLERY SEDGWICK, JR.

FOREWORD BY AMB. THEODORE SEDGWICK

HAMILTON BOOKS
an imprint of
Rowman & Littlefield
Lanham • Boulder • New York • London

Published by Hamilton Books
An imprint of The Rowman & Littlefield Publishing Group, Inc.
4501 Forbes Boulevard, Suite 200, Lanham, Maryland 20706
www.rowman.com

86-90 Paul Street, London EC2A 4NE, United Kingdom

Book design by Annie Langan

British Library Cataloguing in Publication Information Available

Library of Congress Cataloging-in-Publication Data

ISBN 9780761873488 (paper : alk paper) | ISBN 9780761873495 (ebook)

∞™ The paper used in this publication meets the minimum requirements of American National Standard for Information Sciences—Permanence of Paper for Printed Library Materials, ANSI/NISO Z39.48-1992.

Lt. Commander Ellery Sedgwick, Jr.

CONTENTS

FOREWORD

BY AMB. THEODORE SEDGWICK

My Experiences in World War II is Lt. Commander Ellery Sedgwick, Jr.'s account of his service in Naval Intelligence during the war.

Sedgwick foresaw that after Hitler invaded Poland, it was a question of time before the U.S. got into the war, so he applied for a Commission in the Naval Reserve as early as 1939 and was called to active duty in February of 1941. They called him Kilroy because he was everywhere, from Panama and North Africa, to Italy and France, to the Pacific Islands—four continents. He experienced three landings—two in Normandy and the southern coast of France and one in Lingayen in the Philippines.

Sedgwick, who grew up in Boston, Massachusetts, later became a successful businessman in Cleveland, Ohio. He applied this can-do business mentality—*how do you reach your goals?*—to his Naval service. This was often frustrating to him because

ELLERY SEDGWICK, JR's WWII TOUR

Cannes, France

London, England

Plymouth, UK

Utah Beach, Normandy, France

New York, NY, U.S.A

Red Beach, San Raphael, France

Washington, D.C., U.S.A

Naples, Italy

NORTH PACIFIC OCEAN

NORTH ATLANTIC OCEAN

Port Lyautey, Morocco

Algiers, Algeria

Pearl Harbor, Honolulu, Hawaii

Casablanca, Morocco

Oran, Algeria

Panama

SOUTH ATLANTIC OCEAN

Kerama Islands, Okinawa

Lingayen, Philippines

Ulithi Atoll, Caroline Islands

Leyte, Philippines

Manus Island, Papua New Guinea

Bougainville Island, Papua New Guinea

Lae, Papua New Guinea

Guadalcanal

INDIAN OCEAN

LOCATIONS 1941 - 1945

Washington D.C., U.S.A.
Panama
New York, NY, U.S.A.
Port Lyautey, Morocco
Casablanca, Morocco
Oran, Algeria
Algiers, Algeria
Plymouth, UK
Utah Beach, Normandy, France
London, England
Naples, Italy
Red Beach, San Raphael, France

Cannes, France
Panama
Pearl Harbor, Honolulu, Hawaii
Guadalcanal, Solomon Islands
Bougainville Island, Papua New Guinea
Lae, Papua New Guinea
Manus Island, Papua New Guinea
Lingayen, Philippines
Leyte, Philippines
Ulithi Atoll, Caroline Islands
Kerama Islands, Okinawa

all too often his Navy superiors believed that the Army was a more important enemy than the Germans and Japanese.

In reading his account, he made two significant contributions to the war effort. First, he analyzed the gradients of the shorelines at Normandy and Southern France, as well as in the Pacific, to see where the optimum places were to land. In fact, he wrote parts of the plans for the Normandy invasion. Second, in the Pacific Theater, he is credited by Naval historian Samuel Eliot Morrison as being the leading expert on Japanese Kamikaze pilots. Typically, his superiors attempted to block his efforts to share his knowledge and advice widely in the Navy.

As one of his three sons, he never spoke much about the war to us, or to our sister. However, he did seem to run into a lot of people he knew in his global peregrinations, and he kept up with many of them for many decades after the war.

Sedgwick died of a heart attack at age 82 in 1991. His evaluations of the captains and admirals he worked for in the Navy—both good and bad—will be of interest to scholars and avid readers of the role of Naval Intelligence in World War II.

— Amb. Theodore "Tod" Sedgwick

INTRODUCTION

At the instigation of my wife, and with the thought that our children might someday find interest in these notes, I am setting down here a brief review of my personal observations and activities in WWII. Many of the details of actions and the names of places in command are already lost from my poor memory, and so this can in no way be considered a historical record, but will merely touch on the highlights of my own personal experiences.

In 1939 when Germany invaded Poland, and England declared war, it became apparent that we would eventually have to go in. I therefore made application for a commission in the Naval Reserve in the field of Intelligence. This did not come through until October of 1940, when I was taken in as a Lieutenant, Junior Grade. In February of 1941, I was called to active duty within an assignment at the 15th naval district, Panama Canal Zone. In as much as I had pneumonia in Thomasville, Ga., at that time, the assignment had to be deferred. I was next called up on June 24, 1941, seven weeks after my marriage. Let me point out that prior to this first active assignment, I had no knowledge or training in Navy ways or functioning in general, or intelligence duties in partic-ular. However, looking back at that time, I could honestly say that no one else, either of high or low rank in the Navy had any real knowledge of the purpose and function of the Intelli-gence. It required the experience of the entire war to produce a sound and constructive pattern. My first orders took me to Washington for a two-week period of indoctrination. All this amounted to was going around the Office of Naval Intelligence (ONI) on my own, and trying to find out what was going on, (which certainly did not seem to be very much, although a lot of new young officers were milling around looking very busy).

PANAMA

While I was in Washington, I made arrangements for transportation by a Navy transport for Sis[1] and myself to Panama. As an example of my ignorance of Navy regulations, I asked the officer in charge whether or not there would be a bar on our ship. He had also recently joined and had to consult several others before finding out that there was a very long standing rule on the subject of barring all liquor on U.S. Naval ships. Our trip to Panama was in the order of a cruise. We stopped at Bermuda; Guantánamo, Cuba; San Juan, Puerto Rico; and the Virgin Islands. During this time, we made the acquaintances of several young officers who were to become good friends and work in the same organization with me. When we arrived we were met by George Merryweather at Cristobel and went over on the train to Bilbao where the naval headquarters were. George had gotten an apartment for us, and in the next few days we had obtained all the essentials to start up housekeeping.

[1] Ellery Sedgwick Jr.'s wife, Elizabeth Wade Sedgwick

I reported to headquarters the next day and met my boss, Captain Dillan, a hard-bitten, grouchy old man who had been retired and called back for the emergency. I think underneath, he had a kind heart, but his theory was to break the new officers in the hard way, give them no responsibility, bark at them always, and bite their heads off at every opportunity. I am afraid he was not a very bright man and spent more time and effort fighting for his prerogative than implanting a sound intelligence program. This was doubly true, however, of his commanding officer, Rear Admiral Sadler, Commandant of the district. Sadler was a nice enough old man with a lot of pomp and dignity, but his whole obsession was fighting against the Army over control of the isthmus, which had been laid down by the chiefs of staff in Washington, and trying to keep a completely independent Navy.[2] His socially conscious wife abetted him in his endeavors. He was a tin God, and like other admirals at that time, did not even take the steps and measures that were available to him to attempt obtaining security against an attack. Fortunately it never came. Almost all my work during my duty in Panama was of an unimportant and rather uninteresting nature. The same applied to almost all the 30 other Intelligence officers.

As I think back, I honestly believe without any feeling of self pride or conceit, that there have been many days since that I have accomplished more in a day than our Intelligence section

---

[2] Indeed, a document in the FDR Library labeled "Secret" indicates that Rear Admiral F.H. Sadler was relieved of his command on April 15, 1942.

His Commander Paul F. Foster had recommended some changes in the organization of the Intelligence operations in the Caribbean but Sadler rejected them "on the grounds, among others, that to accept them would aid the Army in its alleged plot to gain and retain control of Naval Aviation."

did in a year in Panama. We may have served our purpose though, because there was no successful sabotage or any attempt for that matter, and we did build up a wonderful file on suspicious characters. However, life was far from dull. The hours were very short until December 7th, and we made many close friends. Many officers also had their wives there, and the group as a whole was about as fine of a bunch as one would meet anywhere. At least a half-dozen I still include as my closest friends. There was a little golf and tennis, an occasional dinner and a good many small parties which made life very pleasant. Given the heat and humidity being so terrific, we had to take life pretty easily. Late in the summer we moved from our apartment in town to the other half of the house in which George was living. It was a few miles out and right on the Pacific where we could watch the magnificent sunsets while we ate dinner and enjoyed a little more breeze. A nice garden full of bougainvillea and a green lawn with palm trees on the edge surrounded the house, and life was altogether delightful. On December 7th, I was preparing to go on a cruise to the Galapagos Islands and had visited the old four-stack destroyer that was to give me a bit of sea experience. Back home for lunch with Sis, I got a telephone call from headquarters saying to "get down there in a hurry." Then the news was out on the radio. The next 48 hours were quite a melee. The several intelligence sections, primarily the army G-2, rounded up all Japanese, Germans, and Italians and other suspects, and put them in pens. The wife of one of the high naval officers jumped under the bed when she heard the news, and others I heard of, barricaded themselves with sandbags under their houses. Everyone speculated on the actual extent of damage to our fleet at Pearl Harbor and then guessed the situation as bad as it was. All of us changed from civilian clothes to uniforms. I remember having the Navy insulted by more than one merchant ship captain whom I visited to make routine checks, because they had been caught flat-footed. On an investigation of a little tuna fish boat, I discovered five Japanese hiding below, and had them brought in. They may have been harmless fishermen, but maybe not. We started organizing local defense and I had charge of a 50-caliber machine gun team on the roof of headquarters to be manned in case of air raids. I had occasion to see later on, in the other parts of the world, how totally ineffective these weapons would have been against an airplane. The overall defense of the canal was pathetic and it was indeed fortunate that the Japanese did not strike there. General Andrews[3] who was in overall charge, did an excellent job with what he had, but he had very little, probably not more than 10 or 20 first line bombers and 25 to 50 fighters. I heard there were not more than 2,000 mobile troops, not including guards, available for defense against a landing. The Navy, which did not do the best with what it had, but merely yelled for more, had, I think, four 20-year-old destroyers, one old gun boat, several yard patrol craft, and six old submarines. But the Japanese did not strike and we only had one air raid alarm, which later proved to be unfounded. From an Intelligence standpoint, one of the

---

[3] Lt. Gen. Frank M. Andrews at this time was Commander of the Caribbean Defense Command, charged with defending the southern approaches to the U.S. including the Panama Canal. In 1942, he became Commander of all U.S. forces in the Middle East, where he helped defeat Rommel's Afrika Korps. In 1943 he became Commander of all U.S. forces in the European Theater of Operations. Gen. Henry H. "Hap" Arnold, commander of Army Air Forces, said in his memoirs he believed that Andrews would have been given command of the Allied invasion of Europe. Tragically, he died in a crash of a B-24 in Iceland. Andrews Air Force Base in Maryland is named in his honor.

principal dangers came from German-operated planes coming from South America. Germans controlled three or four airlines there, and employed some 300 pilots, most of whom were German nationals. A study of this situation constituted one of my principal assignments. However, the three principally involved countries in South America—Colombia, Venezuela, and Ecuador—were attentive to the suggestions of the U.S. and cooperated in eliminating the threat by closing the airlines or taking them over.

Shortly after Pearl Harbor Day, the talks centered around when our wives would be evacuated home. The order soon came and early in February, Sis flew off. The separation was heartbreaking, but I felt a little easier in my mind because one could not tell in those early months what might come. The real threat was not eliminated until after the Battle of Midway about June 3, 1942. After Sis left, I moved in and lived in an apartment with Frank Akers, whose wife had also gone. Very shortly, I had to move a second time to one of the family houses on the Naval reservation. My work after the war started did not increase in interest or importance. One of my chief interests, however, was watching the traffic of our great warships through the canal. Of course, this was kept terribly secret, but in line with one of my jobs, I knew approximately when a great many convoys were coming through and I could drive down near one of the big locks and wait. It was a stirring experience to see our new ships and the pride of our Navy on their way through to the big action in the Pacific. They were inspiring with their neat, efficient, and tremendously powerful appearance. They were bristling with guns, bigger than anything I had seen in pictures. That was a real Navy and they were on their way to war. There was, as I recall, the *Saratoga, Washington, North Carolina, Essex, South Dakota*, and many others, all magnificent in themselves and a source of great confidence to the spectator. There were also occasional great convoys of troop ships. Each ship was jammed to the gunnels, and the decks covered with tiers of bunks, four deep. My friend Dave Wier in the Lakeside Hospital Unit was in one of the early convoys about January of 1942. I went aboard his ship, a former liner, and found 52 officers living in three rooms which were designed for three passengers each. They all had bad colds from the spotty issue of cold weather clothing for this mid-winter trip. I collected a couple of cases of liquor from the officer's club, which was all I could lay my hands on that Sunday morning, and got a grateful letter of thanks later from Australia. One factor that disturbed us in Intelligence was the fact that in spite of the great secrecy that surrounded these movements, the German radio in Panama would invariably announce in English the composition of the convoys almost before they were out of our sight in the Pacific. Of course it was impossible to keep the casual observer from seeing the ships as they went through the canal. But there was 100% censorship of mail, radio, and telephone for 72 hours after these movements. Several of us were assigned to investigate this situation to find the leaks. I am not at all sure that we ever did, but we made several suggestions which were acted on and the net result was that the German radio discontinued their announcements. For one thing, we held up coded diplomatic radio messages from the Spanish and other legations in Panama City. We also monitored the local Panamanian radio station, and had one suspected employee discharged.

We permitted only certain official and urgent plane passenger traffic out of the zone for forty-eight hours after an important convoy movement.

Probably the greatest problem faced by the naval command in Panama was the submarine menace in the Caribbean. There were several reports of Japanese subs on the Pacific side, but none of these proved to be found in fact. The first German subs were reported in January of 1942 in the Caribbean and they were present with greater and greater frequency until May and June. I believe there were over 60 of our ships sunk in those two months alone, with a record of nine down in a single day. Of course we were very ill-prepared to meet the situation with so few escort vessels and patrol planes. Our techniques and anti-submarine devices were in the kindergarten stage. Throughout my almost two years in Panama, the Naval forces of the Panama sea frontier did not successfully attack or sink a single German sub. Ironically, I am sorry to report that two of our own subs were lost, one by accidental collision, the other by internal explosion or gas fumes. A French sub, the world's largest, was also sunk by accidental collision. However, as we were allocated more and more escort vessels and patrol planes in the latter half of '42, the German subs had a tougher time and their hunting was not as easy. Also, our information as to the positions of the subs increased and we developed a fairly accurate picture of their movement, so convoys could be routed to avoid them. Much of this information came from intelligence forces, and some from patrol planes. Sub positions were plotted out with great care 24-hours a day by the Intelligence Section. I believe this function was about the most useful we performed, although I had no direct connection with it. There was a common belief that the German subs were being secretly supplied with water provisions and fuel by caches (or with assistance of collaborators) along the shores of the Caribbean. There must have been easily 50-75 such reports received by our section. All of these were investigated either by us or by U.S. Intelligence Officers in other Central American countries. I made one or two such investigations and can say that the help of the United Fruit Co. representatives was invaluable in following the reports down. They knew the country, communities, and people to an extent we could not approach. There was not a single report that was founded on fact. They had the origin in rumor and stories, which spread rapidly, and were greatly embellished with the telling. Another factor that led us to examine the reports so carefully was that the U.S. did not appreciate the endurance abilities of the German subs. They had a longer range and a greater capacity for carrying supplies and people than we had dreamed possible. A seven-week cruise was commonplace for them; two weeks over, three weeks of patrolling, and two weeks back. I am convinced from our experience that there was no resupply of German subs in our section, or for that matter, on our side of the Atlantic.

In August of 1942 having been on duty over 12 months, I was eligible for a month's leave in the States. However, because of the heavy volume of official travel, we were not allowed to use Pan American Airways, which had the only flights going up. There were no commercial ships either. The only alternative seemed to be seven or eight Navy ships going to the East Coast. This would use up half my leave, so I became quite desperate. I discovered, however, that Taca Airlines, a small concern operating mostly contract runs in Central America, was to open a schedule to Panama from Central American countries. They could take me on their first test run to San Jose, Costa Rica. I telephoned my good friend there, Woody Ober, Naval Attaché and he thought he could help me further. So, off I went. I spent a delightful day in San Jose with Obers, and with their assistance, did get a ride in a Trimotor Ford plane to Tegucigalpa, Honduras. There, my situation looked pretty bleak. After I had been at the tiny airport about an hour, a man came in with a bunch of small paper packages that seemed very heavy. He was followed by two guards. It didn't take long to find out that he was a gold miner and was taking some of his gold to the U.S. by special chartered plane. I found occasion to introduce and identify myself as a Naval Intelligence Officer and asked if I could accompany him to Miami. His plane, a new Lockheed twin engine, arrived shortly and we were in Miami in a few hours. My feeling of jubilation upon arriving on American soil was tremendous, partly, of course, because the chance of getting stuck in some Central American country en route had been very considerable. From Miami I got navy transport and commercial planes to take me home in short order. It was then that I saw my three-month-old son, Ellery,[4] for the first time. It was a thrill matched only by seeing my wife again.

Before I conclude these words about my time in Panama, I will make a few comments on the country. Almost its only asset or resource is the canal; and except for a very few ranches and a couple of tiny villages, all the life is centered about The Zone.

[4] Ellery Sedgwick III

There are wild tribes of certain Indians in parts of the south, and only two roads in the whole country. One goes 40 miles south along the coast, and the other up the western coast to the border. The country is quite mountainous and very green from the heavy rainfall. Many parts have up to 200 inches of rainfall a year. Near this zone during the rainy season, it will rain each afternoon for about an hour in torrents. The cities were filthy and overflowing with vice. About $5,000 worth of jewelry that George Merryweather had given his wife was stolen one morning from our double house. The house, incidentally, was rented from Arnulfo Arias, the President of the country. He was a great fancier of women, and early in 1942, he could not resist the temptation of chasing one to Cuba. The opposition party took advantage of his departure to invoke a constitutional provision which prohibited the President from leaving the country without Congressional permission. A minor revolution took place with almost no bloodshed and Arnulfo was out of a job. This was fortunate for the U.S. because he was pro-Axis in word and deed and had tried to block us at every turn. I am convinced, however, that this coup d'etat was not instigated by the U.S. Subsequently, we concluded a new treaty with Panama that gave us the air field sites and other considerations that we wanted, but in return for a large price. The Zone is only 10 miles wide and not nearly adequate in itself to contain airfields, AA gun and radar sites, searchlights, and for that matter, the coast-to-coast motor highway. Regarding the latter, I found it difficult to believe that before 1943 we had no motor road across the Ismus (Isthmus), only a single-track antiquated railroad. From the standpoint of military security, this seemed inexcusable because, as even a schoolboy knows, the essence of modern war is mobility.

But, enough of Panama. I was pretty well fed up with the idle and uneventful life there when I went on my first leave to the States. I stopped off in Washington and asked for another assignment, preferably at sea, but they refused me, and back I went. However, early the following year, I put in another written request to the advanced Naval Intelligence School in New York, which seemed to be a stepping stone to more interesting duty. The request was accepted. I was released in March and met Sis for a wonderful few days in Virginia before starting school in New York.

NEW YORK & WASHINGTON

I worked quite hard at the Advanced Naval Intelligence School in New York, but did not end up head of the class of some 150 officers. Sis and I had a nice little apartment close by and we had an altogether enjoyable time, even though I had to get to school at the unearthly hour of 6 a.m. Little El was with us too, which kept things humming.

The purpose of this school was to teach us the procedures, techniques, and background for Operational Intelligence, preparatory to assignment abroad or afloat. A word here about counterintelligence. Up to this time I had been doing mostly counterintelligence work, which was trying to track down the enemies' agents and sympathizers and providing security for our own. In operational and combat intelligence, you work directly with and for your armed forces, providing them with all possible information about the enemy, his capabilities, and his intentions. One of the most interesting courses at the school was in anti-submarine warfare. We learned first-hand all of the modern techniques for attacking them and spent a night on patrol outside of New York Harbor. We also studied a lot of geography of the areas of operation. I had trouble with the course in navigation, even though I had taken a three-month course in Panama. The lecturers came down from the Naval War College at Newport and talked to us on a variety of subjects, including the great naval battles of the war. These might have been fascinating, but the regular Naval officers who gave them made them as dull as dishwater. There was also a course in photographic interpretation given by a man named Turkette, who was later to work with me in several operations. The course was the study of matched aerial photographs with the aid of stereoscope, which was to become an absolutely invaluable source of information, particularly in connection with amphibious operations. There were several other courses, but the general impression that I formed was that the whole subject of Operational Intelligence was relatively undeveloped and in its infancy. I felt also that it was of tremendous importance and I was 100% sold on its value. It was almost entirely untried and almost all Navy commanders were prejudiced against it, and for that reason, they would not accept or practice it. Intelligence Officers assigned to them were treated with a certain amount of ridicule and given the job of laundry superintendent, head of the shop store, or the like. Almost universally they were not afforded the proper opportunity for practicing what they had been studying, or what they were intended for. This generally did not boost the morale of Naval Intelligence officers. However, all one had to do to maintain his convictions for the value of intelligence was to think of some of the hideous blunders made by regular naval officers who did not make proper use of the available information on the enemy. The Battle of Savo Island where we lost four cruisers, three destroyers, and hundreds and hundreds of lives at a crucial time in our history, is an outstanding example of this. It was the day after our first landing on Guadalcanal and the first cruisers and some destroyers were guarding the transports and beach head. A reconnaissance plane spotted the Japanese force early in the morning. The information was delayed in getting through, but did arrive several hours before they struck. However, it was either ignored or misinterpreted, for the Japanese struck about midnight and our force was all but annihilated. It was about the darkest moment for our high command in the Naval War. An intelligence officer receiving this information would not have failed to have alerted his commanding officer to the danger of the situation, but there was no intelligence officer in that force.

The greatest event of the two months at the school was when Commander Baldwin and Lieutenant Commander Thayer, who had started the school in connection with their operational intelligence program, came up to interview us all in regard to future assignments. The interview with each officer lasted less than five minutes, but in as much as it determined where he would spend the next two or more years, it was pretty important. I was naturally trying to make my best impression and as a result made a very poor one. It was the first time I had met these gentlemen, who I was to be closely associated with later. I made a strong plea for duty afloat, but they thought it best to look me over a bit more thoroughly first, and I was subsequently assigned to Baldwin's office in Washington on a temporary basis. This was a considerable blow, but it did mean that I would be with my family a bit longer.

My wife will testify that I was pretty hard to live with in Washington, and pretty unhappy. But looking back, I think my six months there gave me a much broader picture of the functioning of the services than I would have gotten otherwise. I worked in the small Operational Intelligence section, which was part of the Office of Naval Intelligence. I sensed immediately that ONI was torn with petty intrigue and friction and that our section was the very center of it. All other section heads resented us because we were new and were taking a more prominent position in the whole organization. As an example, one day I was having routine conversations with another section head in connection with my work when the Naval captain in charge of the entire branch called me into his office and gave me HELL for interfering in matters that I had no business with. I was flabbergasted at the pettiness of his charges and that he would trump up insignificant excuses to pick a quarrel with me. In the middle of his castigation, the door opened and in came Commander Baldwin to my defense. In his cool, suave manner, he talked to the captain and settled the whole subject very quickly, showing that I was entirely within my rights, and the captain did not have a leg to stand on. I could see the captain smarting under this reverse, and he would continue plotting retaliation. I saw this type of situation on every side, and it was appalling, but true, to think that there were a number of high officials much more interested in enhancing their own position and keeping others down than in prosecuting the war.

This not only went on in ONI, but also between that office and other intelligence agencies in Washington. Just as in Panama, the three principal intelligence agencies were terribly concerned with their jurisdiction and prerogatives and were very jealous of each other. I remember once arranging a conference for a few of our officers with the officials of the Office of Strategic Services (OSS) in an attempt to bring about a greater understanding of each others' functions. It was all arranged when the director of Naval Intelligence, an Admiral, got wind of it and stopped it. I finally got it arranged again, but only on the condition that he himself sit in on the conference to make sure that they did not put anything over on us. My job was principally one of planning operational intelligence activities in various theaters of war and setting up organizations to accomplish these missions. Baldwin had unusual energy and sensed, as I did, the great importance of getting the program going. He was always full of ideas and had the executive ability to put them across. However, beside the obstacles imposed by the internal political intrigue, there was endless routine red tape. Unless you experience yourself the working of a great bureaucracy, it is not possible to appreciate just what red tape means. I recall that in connection with setting up an organization in England, my letter outlining the plan had to be initialed by 12 section heads and other officers before being signed by the Admiral. Each one of them had some objection and suggestions for changes, even if they didn't. The time involved in discussing it with all of them consumed about a week. I think I rewrote that letter several times and was probably fortunate in getting it through at all. This is by no means an unusual example. It is unnecessary to elaborate on how this process slows down the accomplishment of all work to a crawl. Baldwin was a master at cutting through red tape whenever possible, and much of his program was accomplished by his close tie to the assistant director of Naval Intelligence, Captain Zacharias.[5] The captain was a brilliant and very energetic regular Naval officer who saw the importance of Baldwin's work. Even he, however, had to tread pretty carefully to avoid crossing up and offending the stodgy dull old Admiral.

My most important job in Washington was working together with Bill Ladd in the organization of the Naval Intelligence group in England. We worked well together and mapped out, in considerable detail, a plan which was subsequently accepted in all its major aspects. We also hand-picked almost all the personnel. I had an opportunity later, when I was in England, to see the organization at work in almost the manner we had planned. I was told by the Naval captain in charge that it had been very effective. This was the only source of satisfaction I got from any of my work in Washington.

Another plan, which I worked on a little, was an attempt to provide a world-wide joint Intelligence Organization. Rather than have overlapping authority and duplication of effort of the four or five information gathering agencies in all the war theaters, it seemed reasonable to install a unified organization wherein the Army, Navy, State Department, Office of War Information, and OSS, could each have their own sphere of operation and exchange their information with the other interested agencies in the field. However, although Baldwin

[5] Rear Admiral Ellis Mark Zacharias Sr. commanded a number of battleships during his career. He was a visionary who after the war, to prevent squabbling between the intelligence services, developed plans to restructure and centralize military intelligence to under the organizational name Joint Intelligence Agency. His plans would not be realized until 1961 when the Defense Intelligence Agency was formed.

and others spent a great deal of effort on this, the project was pretty much a complete failure. It came down again to rivalry and jealousy between the services. They could not and would not cooperate, regardless of directives from Washington. It was the same in Algiers, Cairo, and India. During the summer, the Baldwin program was going along at a pretty good pace. A great many officers were selected and trained for billets with the fleet and overseas. A lot of these men, having gotten the germ of an idea, went out and did splendid jobs in the field, and I subsequently came across their trails all over the world. Many were side-tracked by commanding officers who knew nothing about intelligence functions, but others pushed on and did a whale of a good job for which they were commended and decorated. For instance, a young friend from Panama, Joe Hadlam, who had gone to the school with me, went to the South Pacific with a PT squadron. They found his many services invaluable and he was awarded the bronze star. Then there was Ed Reddon, also of Panama, who was decorated for a very daring reconnaissance mission which brought back invaluable information from one of the Solomon Islands shortly before our troops landed. There were several others, who in Sicily, landed with the first troops and dynamited a safe in Italian headquarters to find priceless documents revealing enemy naval dispositions and enemy mine fields in the Mediterranean. There were many others all of them, of course, deserve full credit—but had it not been for Baldwin and Thayer's program and impetus, they never would have had a chance to show results.

In the early fall, Baldwin was overdue to take a trip to visit and observe some of the activities he had set up. The day he left by plane, Captain Zacharias was removed from his position of assistant director of Naval Intelligence. I do not have the exact facts, but I can say with conviction that it was because he had stepped on the toes of higher-ups by his advanced and progressive ideas. The Admiral, encouraged by most of his subordinates, took the first opportunity to have him transferred. There is no doubt in my mind, and with my years of intelligence in and out of Washington, I can speak with as much authority as anyone, that Zacharias did more for naval Intelligence than any regular naval officer, or officer of comparable or higher rank, during the war. It is shocking to think that this capable and brilliant officer who accomplished every task assigned with eminence was never promoted to Admiral. He was too smart for the Annapolis boys.

To get back, the day after he was fired, the old guard, taking advantage of Baldwin's absence and the loss of his friend in court, called a meeting of the planning board, and abolished his section. They had been waiting for this moment for a long time and the situation was perfect for them. As a matter of fact, it took two or three days to accomplish it according to the book, and then it was approved by the Admiral. No one, not Thayer or myself or any of his friends and followers were allowed to come to his aid and give testimony at the meetings. It was the rankest kind of bureaucracy and bureaucratic intrigue that I can conceive of. They merely resented his presence and program in the organization and knifed him when his back was turned. Let me say a word here as to who these old guards were. They were Captain Perry, Kishner, Baltasi, and others, including old Admiral Crane who were dull, impotent, and unimaginative. To the great misfortune of ONI, they had been consigned a lot of deadwood, regular

Naval officers for whom they could not quite find a place elsewhere. This was typical of the navy attitude towards intelligence in the early years of the war. It just didn't matter who you stuck in these places because they couldn't do any harm. These men liked their jobs and didn't appreciate any disturbing elements.

There were only three other officers in the Operational Intelligence section, but it put us all out on our ear. In my case, however, it so happened that I had been selected to make a trip to North Africa to study and report on the operation of a joint intelligence activity in Algiers and Iran, as well as to carry some secret documents both ways.

I had my ticket by air and my orders and only had to wait for a seat on the plane. In the general confusion, and while the old guards were licking their chops, they forgot to cancel my orders. Without our section there was no point of my trip, but I laid low for a few days and kept checking on my plane. They finally had a seat for me and I shoved off confident that a naval officer could never be criticized for carrying out orders. This trip was terribly interesting for me and gave me a little closer and more realistic picture of the war. I left at the end of September on an American Export Airlines plane, with the first stop at Atwood, Newfoundland. We had engine trouble on the way up and one motor cut out in a bad storm. We landed safely, however, and after repairs, took off for Ireland. This second lap in a four-motored seat plane took about fourteen hours over the ocean. Our berths were made up by the hostess, and I slept like a baby for nine hours on the sponge rubber mattress. Ireland was even greener than the storybooks say and we came down on the river near Toynes. Incidentally, I was dressed as a civilian because that country being neutral could not allow military traffic. This did not fool the Irish, but they passed it off with a wink. We came in there on three motors also, and it took a day to repair. I spent the day at a delightful inn and walking about the countryside. Then on to North Africa. We landed on the river at Port Lyaute in French Morocco. It is a barren land with almost no vegetation and the hills and mountains along the coast are all sandstone. We had a small Army and Navy Air Force base at Lyaute.

My itinerary was entirely my own, so I thought I would visit Casablanca first. My orders specified no particular places to stop, but I had a high travel priority, so I got out on the first plane. It was less than an hour's run to Casablanca. The town with its white houses neatly laid out, its gardens and palm lined streets, stood out from the bleak desert about it. I had forgotten to change my civilian suit, so when I landed I was approached and questioned by local authorities while I identified myself. I called Naval Headquarters and a jeep came out for me. The city was very pleasant and I was excited to be in this foreign country. The Navy put me up in a good room in a hotel they had taken over, and I spent the evening talking to intelligence officers stationed there to whom I introduced myself. They had their troubles around conflict of authority between the services, but they lived well, and were, I thought, doing a pretty good job.

The next day I went out to the airport again and found many waiting for planes, although few planes were expected. Again, with my priority, I got on the first plane and was the only passenger aboard because it was carrying high-priority aircraft

FRENCH MOROCCO

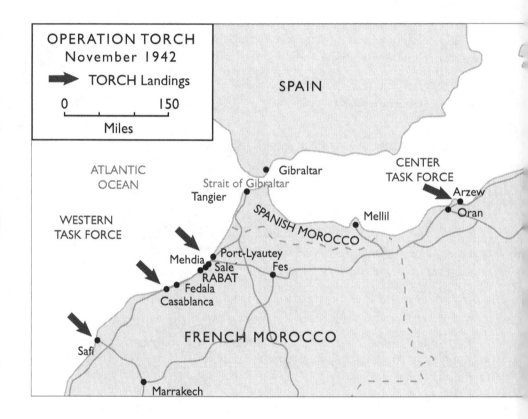

OPERATION TORCH
November 1942

TORCH Landings

0   150
Miles

SPAIN

ATLANTIC
OCEAN

CENTER
TASK FORCE

Gibraltar

Strait of Gibraltar

Arzew

Tangier

Mellil

Oran

WESTERN
TASK FORCE

SPANISH MOROCCO

Port-Lyautey

Mehdia

Sale

Fes

RABAT

Fedala

Casablanca

FRENCH MOROCCO

Safi

Marrakech

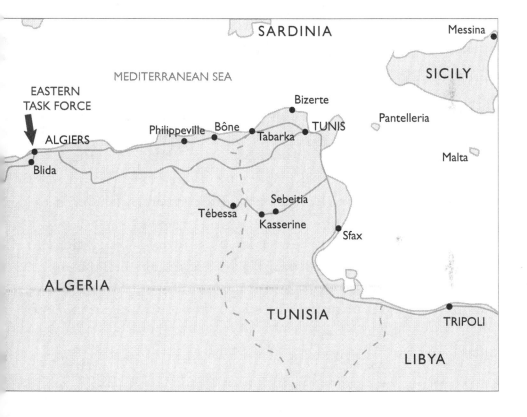

engine parts. For four hours we flew over the desert and barren mountains and came down in Oran, which was our largest port in Africa at that time. It was a foul city with no pleasant physical aspects about it. The streets were filthy and the people filthier, but the docks were terribly interesting and teaming with activity. Gun tanks, planes, and supplies of all kinds poured off the ships and into the stockpiles, and then were taken away by truck. There must have been almost a mile of docks there by the city and all in good condition. We were using Italian prisoners as stevedores and they were very good. Better, in fact, than our own troops who hated the work. An acquaintance I made drove me out to El Kebir which is a beautiful natural harbor west of the city, which we used as a fleet anchorage.

I left Oran as soon as I had obtained the information I wanted concerning the functions of the intelligence and organization. My next stop was Algiers. It was the capital for all of the Allies in North Africa, and for that matter, the Mediterranean. General De Gaulle was there and also Generals Alexander,[6] Clark,[7] Tedder,[8] and many others. One of the most striking things about the city was the constant procession of troops of all descriptions

[6] Field Marshall Harold Alexander, 1st Earl of Tunis, oversaw the final stages of the evacuation from Dunkirk and served as Commander-in-Chief of the Middle East. Later in the war, he became Supreme Allied Commander Mediterranean and after the war served as Governor General of Canada and British Minister of Defense under Churchill.

[7] In October 1942, General Mark Clark was appointed deputy to Gen. Eisenhower for the Mediterranean Theater of Operations. He made a secret visit to French North Africa to meet with pro-Allied officers of the Vichy French forces. Churchill took a shine to him, calling him "The American Eagle."

[8] Marshall of the Royal Air Force, Arthur William Tedder, 1st Baron Tedder, commanded the RAF Middle East Command and later the Mediterranean Allied Air Forces. He later became Deputy Supreme Commander of the Normandy invasion under Eisenhower and signed the German surrender for Eisenhower.

and nationalities that you would see wherever you went. There were not only the great camps of Americans, British, and French, but one saw Poles, Ethiopians, Dutch, Czechs, and most extraordinary of all, French Equatorial Colonels with long robes, turbans, and bare feet, carrying every kind of weapon imaginable. This also gave you a picture of the job involved in trying to consolidate a command in bringing all the troops there for a common task. My principal interest in North Africa lay in this city, and I spent about a week there. It was not hard to see why our joint intelligence organization was not functioning very smoothly. The first time I saw him, the Navy captain in charge talked to me for about three hours about all of the underhanded things his army opposite number was doing and how he lacked support from Washington. My first impression was substantiated by other interviews, that both officers, particularly this captain, were much more concerned about their prerogatives than anything else.

While in Algiers, I had the good fortune of running into an old friend who was executive officer of a destroyer which was shortly to sail with a small convoy from Palermo to Salerno, Italy, where we had just made an amphibious landing and where the fighting was very heavy. He said that if I could get myself to Palermo within 24 hours, I could make the trip with him. I went out to Algiers airport and started contacting all pilots about to take off to see if I could get a ride. In a few hours, I was successful and got a ride on a freight plane. We made one stop at Bigente and I got my first glimpse of real destruction. The town had been absolutely leveled and the docks destroyed. There was hardly a wall of a building standing.

We arrived at Palermo at dusk and it was a lovely site. I had often heard of the city, but never had been there. With some difficulty I found the ship that evening and went aboard. At six the next morning, the convoy pulled out and I was on my first excursion into a combat zone. There were two destroyers, two destroyer escorts, and about 15 landing ship tanks. The escorts made frequent turns and changes of speed, but the trip was made without incident. Shortly after we arrived at the beachhead and were screening the ships, the alarm sounded and all hands were called to general quarters. I saw several of our planes pass over high, then the anti-aircraft guns on shore opened up. Finally, the heavy guns of our own and other ships started. I was on deck, but all I could see was some tiny specks far on the horizon over the hills. They were evidently raiding the beachhead, trying to hit supply dumps, as they did frequently. As night came on, we could also see artillery duels going on between the Germans who held the heights six or eight miles inland and our own forces on shore.

Occasionally, one of the British cruisers offshore would open up when they thought they had an enemy battery spotted. I was pretty excited by all this; as a matter of fact, my eyes were popping and I felt far from being entirely at ease. Everyone on the ship however, was taking it entirely as a matter of course. It struck me then with full-force for the first time, but not the last, what a contrast there was between the lives of these men of the fighting forces, and those in the service who were sitting in Washington, or for that matter, in any non-combat zone. These men were subject to being torpedoed or bombed to instant death at any moment, whereas the others were risking nothing. I have been on both sides and there is a chasm between.

At this particular time, the Germans had unleashed a new and unholy weapon for the first time. It was the radio-controlled rocket bomb, which was guided into its target by the plane which released it. This bomb had sunk the Italian battleship *Roma*, three British cruisers, and put two cruisers of ours, *Brooklyn* and *Columbia*, completely out of action, I think. It had us pretty worried because we had as of yet found no counter defense against it. I was fortunate in not seeing any of these in operation at this time.

The next day I had the opportunity of making a quick trip to shore in a small boat, but did not see much except for a few shells bursting in the distance and a group of wounded soldiers being loaded on an LST (Landing Ship Tank). Their faces were very grave.

Back on the ship we were soon under way, this time convoying some cargo ships to Palermo. The trip was without event and I slept almost all the way. I hitchhiked a ride back to Algiers by Army transport. The only other event of interest I had in North Africa was at the airport as I was leaving Algiers. I had a couple of hours to spend, and was looking for a Red Cross shack with something to eat. I wandered about and came to a likely looking place and walked in. It was empty and I was about to leave when a door opened and in walked an English officer of high rank in a flyer's uniform. I excused myself for the intrusion and told him of my mistake. He was most cordial and asked me to stay for a cup of tea with him. Then he introduced himself by saying, "My name is Tedder"—and it came to me on a flash that this was the great air marshal, Sir Arthur

Tedder.[9] I was stupidly covered with confusion, and after shaking hands with him, beat a hasty retreat.

I had made one or two friends in Algiers, and arranged my schedule to fly back to the States with them. We went to Port Lyaute together and, finding our plane delayed a couple of days, went down to Casablanca where we had a very good time together and bought a few souvenirs. One mistake I think I made was on the night before we left North Africa. I was asleep in the barracks at Port Lyaute when someone came in and yelled out that there was a single seat on the plane going back via Dacar and Belem, Brazil. I should have grabbed the opportunity to go this different route, but I was too sleepy I guess, and let it slip.

The trip to Faynes was smooth and we had a very nice day walking about the Irish countryside. Incidentally, I chatted with several of the local farmers and they had unusual interest in my having lived in Boston. There were at least three or four of them who had several brothers or sisters who had moved there quite a while before, and were chauffeurs, maids, or gardeners of people I knew.

A couple of hours out from Ireland, across the Atlantic, we saw a magnificent sight as we were flying a few hundred feet above water. A formation of eight British destroyer escorts were maneuvering into position to attack a German sub. They turned together with exact precision, fanned out, and let go their depth charges at intervals. It was all timed and executed with perfect synchronization. We were out of sight in a short time, so I cannot tell about the luck they had. We were back in New York on schedule. At about 17:00, I went to Boston for the weekend to

[9] See footnote 8

see my father.[10] When I returned to Washington, I wrote a careful report of my survey. I think it was actually read by some brass hats, because one or two steps were taken shortly thereafter to improve our intelligence set up in North Africa, including the removal of the officer in charge.

I might mention here that I also accomplished one other thing on this trip. Coming back from Palermo to Algiers, I stopped at Malta where most of the Italian fleet, which had just surrendered to us, had been taken. I got from our intelligence officer there his complete report on the fleet, including pictures and detailed data. When I delivered it to Washington, it was the first complete report on this subject they had received. On the way back from Algiers to Port Lyaunte, we stopped at Gibraltar (which was the first time I had ever seen the rock) where there were two Italian ships just taken into custody. I obtained factual reports on these ships, too, and brought them back.

In Washington, I was very anxious not to be assigned a permanent job at ONI because I had been in touch with my friend Bill Ladd,[11] and he had indicated a strong possibility that I might join him in working as a liaison officer for the British Secret Intelligence. This branch of the British service was top notch and had been very effective. Bill was the first U.S. Naval Officer to work with the organization, and his only boss was Admiral Stark,[12] our Navy Commander-in-Chief in Europe. So on returning from

[10] Ellery Sedgwick Sr. was editor and publisher of *The Atlantic Monthly* from 1908 to 1938.

[11] Commander William Ladd was the Office of Naval Intelligence liaison officer with UK Counterintelligence.

[12] Admiral Harold Rainsford Stark was Chief of Naval Operations from 1939 to 1942 and came under criticism for lack of preparation for Pearl Harbor. He was relieved as CNO by Admiral Ernest King, then went to the UK to become Commander of U.S. Naval Forces Europe.

North Africa, I made arrangements to take a temporary job with the joint intelligence collection agency in the Navy Department, knowing that I could not get involved in any permanent job. The work was routine and pretty dull and I did not feel that I was doing very much for the war. In a couple of months, however, a letter came in from Admiral Stark asking for me by name, and asking that I be assigned to him in England. I was a little surprised to hear later that ONI had ignored his request and did not reply to it. A second letter came in a few weeks and then a cable, both asking for me by name. I discontinued my job, then made arrangements for my family to move home, and to let the house we rented go. About a week later, to my absolute astonishment, I learned that ONI had sent Admiral Stark a cable reply saying that my services could not be spared. I protested and pointed out that I was doing absolutely nothing, but to no avail. I never learned what their purpose was, but a few days later, Bob Thayer asked me if I would join a group he was forming to go overseas with an amphibious force. He did not wait for an answer, but the next day asked me if I was ready to leave. I had mixed feelings because I knew not what I was getting into. In any event, I took two weeks leave and went down to visit Sis in Thomasville. We had a sad parting because we had no idea when we might see each other again, or whether I would be in the country when our baby arrived.

Back in Washington, I got my orders which took me to Norfolk. There I got new orders for Fort Pierce in Florida, where I was to learn a few of the essentials of amphibious warfare and get other training at the Scouts and Raider School in combat intelligence technique. They taught us how to paddle a little rubber boat in the surf and in the dark, how to drive an Alligator (an amphibious tank), and a Duwk, a truck which could go 40 m.p.h. on land and six or seven knots in the water. We also had a few exercises in sneaking up on an enemy island at night by running in through the surf with waterproof arms and packs strapped to us. It was all good fun and I had the delightful company of several fellows who were to be with me later on.

All the while at Fort Pierce, I was scheming to try to arrange a quick trip to Thomasville for a last glimpse of Sis, and possibly the new baby expected momentarily. I was never able to realize my plan, however, because we were suddenly recalled to Norfolk with a deadline that prevented stopping on the way. I flew to Washington to avoid the dreadful train trip to Norfolk. I saw Net[13] and Theo[14] and then reported to Norfolk. I remember distinctly my desperate telephone calls to Sis at each place I could put in a call from. Lines were busy and most often calls could not get through. I spent hours and hours by telephone booths, nervously fidgeting without knowledge of little Irene and whether or not she had arrived. My general concern was heightened by the lack of knowledge of what lay ahead of me. I did not know what our assignment would be, what we were really headed for, or when I would next hear from my wife as to how she was.

I was less than two days in Norfolk before our group, some 50 in number, were herded on to a train with considerable secrecy, and sent to New York. While waiting for our baggage to come

---

[13] Henrietta Ellery Sedgwick Lockwood was Sedgwick's older sister.

[14] Theodora Sedgwick Bond was a younger sister who worked for the OSS during WWII, and later married Brig. Gen. William Ross Bond, the only general killed in combat during the Vietnam War.

off the train again, I tried to call Sis. The call went through right away and I had my last talk with her. Irene had not arrived, but the conversation gave me great satisfaction and confidence in Sis's well being.

We were next sent to a pier where we left our baggage and, to everyone's delight, were given the day off. We had a very active day indeed, taking in all that New York had to offer in 12 brief hours. How everyone got back to the pier at the appointed hour of 9 p.m., I'll never know, but they all did—though many of them could hardly walk.

ENGLAND & NORMANDY: D-DAY

Our ship was the *Aquatania*, and we left that night March 14, 1944. There were twelve of us in a cabin designed for three, but it was entirely comfortable and we had a bath to ourselves. We could see right away that we had no escorts and would have to depend on our 25 knots for our security. I don't think any of us were really concerned by this, but we all had our trepidations about the future. It was a new experience for all of us in the group, and we did not know where we were bound, to say nothing of what we would be doing. We knew that we were members of the staff of the commander of Amphibious Group 2, Eleventh Amphibious Force. His name was Admiral Moon.[15] He himself had been on the staff of Admiral King[16] in Washington, and was considered one of the younger, but most promising of the rear

---

[15] Admiral Don P. Moon directed the landings on Utah. Sadly, he committed suicide with his pistol on August 5, 1944. His suicide was attributed to battle fatigue.

[16] Admiral Ernest J. King was Commander-in-Chief of the U.S. Fleet and Chief of Naval Operations during WWII.

admirals. He had flown over to North Africa with Bob Thayer,[17] his staff intelligence officer, and a few others about a month before. Our best combined bet was that we would be the back stop group in the event the high command needed one extra amphibious force in some future and probably subsidiary operation. It was certain that, because of our complete inexperience and the pace with which we were assembled and trained, that we could not be needed for anything very important or very imminent.

There was no substitute for companionship and friendly conversation when your mind is troubled and in doubt about such important matters as this, and an inner circle of us who fell naturally together used to collect over a "jug" and discuss these things. I quickly found out that we all had misgivings about our future, but we did have companionship, and those few "jugs" we had picked up in New York.

The ship was efficiently run and the time passed quickly. Only two meals a day. My sittings were breakfast at 9 a.m. and supper at 6 p.m., and we had two hours of abandoned ship drills each morning. We were told that there were 5,000 on board and I could well believe it, although we were not packed in too tightly. There was frequent change, of course, and we relied on ocean vastness and our speed to get us through. In a few days, we realized by the ship's course that we must be headed for England, and not the Mediterranean. The first land we sighted was Ireland and then two little escorts took us up the Clyde in

[17] Robert H. Thayer had helped investigate the Lindbergh kidnapping. He served as an naval intelligence officer in the Pacific before going to Europe for the Normandy invasion. After the war he was an assistant to John Foster Dulles at the organizing conference for the United Nations in San Francisco and later was appointed by President Eisenhower to Minister to Romania.

Scotland. It was nasty weather, rather misty, and chilly when we went ashore at Greenwich, the port of Glasgow, but we were warm within. A British general gave us a brief speech of welcome while we were still aboard. I remember particularly his words of praise for the combined commander and chief, General Eisenhower, as well as his spirit and cordiality. Ashore in the railroad station, English Red Cross girls gave us hot coffee and donuts and everyone was smiling at us and waving. We felt warm inside and sentimental. A few fellows of our group, including Jerry Casey and Don McNeil, who were excellent singers, broke out with "Annie Laurie" and a few other songs, and crowds came around and cheered us. From the train windows as we pulled out through the town, everyone was waving—little children from the streets and old ladies from the windows of the houses. It was a very touching scene, which I will never forget. It was a warm welcome to a rather dreary shore. We did not know our destination until after the train had pulled out, and then we were told that it would be Plymouth. Our train was efficiently handled and wasted little time en route, except for two stops for supper and breakfast, which we had at stations. Of course, we sat up all night, but I got a bit of sleep.

At Plymouth, we were driven to our camp through the city, which had taken terrific punishment from bombing. Our camp consisted of about 20 Quonset huts, which were placed on two city blocks, which had been completely leveled in the heart of town. The Admiral and his party had arrived a few days before from North Africa and he gave us a little talk, welcoming us and saying that we had no time to waste. The job ahead of us was very large and our time short. He was a large, powerful man, with a pleasant handsome face. He was just 50 years old and abounded with vigor and energy. He was a rather slow and methodical speaker with no sign of brilliance. The story was that he had been picked especially by Admiral King for the job.

We were very shortly to learn what the job was. After breakfast, Bob Thayer took his Intelligence section aside. There were 16 of us in all. I remember my feeling as he pointed out that all of us had previously spent much of our time behind desks in some safe spot far removed from the war, but that now we were really going to be in it, and a part of it. We were to be a vital part of the great invasion of the Continent that was being so much talked and written about on both sides of the Atlantic. Then in typical Thayer fashion he said, "I hope you fellows aren't tired, because tomorrow you go out on a big, full-scale rehearsal, and I don't think you'll get much sleep for a few days." That afternoon he got permission from the Admiral to tell me the details of the invasion. As he pointed out on the maps where and how we would land, I could hardly believe my eyes or ears because this was the thing that I, and everybody else in the world, were speculating and dreaming about. The secret was beyond price with hundreds of thousands of lives and billions of dollars involved. All would be lost if at the Dieppe raid the secret got out.

The assault was to be along about 90 miles of coast in the Bay of the Seine. Five assault forces were to be involved—two British, one Canadian, and two American—with, as I recall, each force putting ashore about 30,000 men the first day and building up rapidly over the next few days. Our own beaches were the furthest to the west along the Cherbourg Peninsula, opposite Sainte-Mère-Église. The ground immediately behind our low lying flat beaches was very marshy, which formed an almost impenetrable natural obstacle. For this reason, it was planned to drop our two airborne divisions behind the marshes a few hours before the main landing. These were the highlights and each subsequent day I was to learn much more of the details.

That evening we were working in a Quonset hut studying and preparing plans for the rehearsal to be held the next day, when the air alarm sounded and we witnessed our first German raid. Many search lights were piercing the sky and then the anti-aircraft broke loose. We had not been drilled in what we should do, so we put on our helmets and watched. Several bombs dropped and you could hear them whistle when they went off. They sounded pretty close but that was to untrained ears, because as we found out the next day, they fell half a mile or so away.

The next day I had an amusing and interesting experience. I was assigned to a liaison officer on a British cruiser for the exercise. As I came alongside in a small boat and was about to go up the ladder, I picked up my bag and all my odds and ends of packages when a petty officer said, "I believe they are preparing to pipe you aboard, sir. I will take your belongings up." Being democratic and ignorant of the British courtesies, I declined his assistance and lumbered up the gangway with all of my things. About six steps from the top, the pipes started and blew shrilly until I was on the quarter-deck. There I found four officers, including the executive officer waiting to receive me. I knew nothing about the formal procedures aboard ship at that time and nothing about the British procedures. I was therefore in a great state of embarrassment as to what to do. The only solution I could think of was to drop everything and salute everyone in sight, as well as the Union Jack. This seemed to get by, but was far from correct. I was assigned a good cabin and my "boy" came immediately with a pitcher of hot water. It was an older cruiser with none of the modern conveniences. On my way to the ward-room for supper, I was interested in how the men slept in ham-mocks hung anywhere and everywhere. Over several drinks, the ice was broken and I enjoyed myself.

Next morning my boy woke me up at 4 a.m. with a cup of tea. We were underway and approaching the rehearsal area. This was a strip of some 20 square miles on the southern coast from which they had evacuated all inhabitants. I found my way in the dark to the bridge with some difficulty, and tried to remain in the dark, or at least well out of the way, throughout the exercise. You see, I knew almost nothing about amphibious warfare or, for that matter, ship tactics, etc., and as a representative of the Admiral of the force, everyone supposed that I would be a fund of knowl-edge. I had a mighty difficult time that morning to sidetrack all the questions that were put to me. I had not even had time to read the plan of operation and I certainly felt foolish at times.

Our bombardment started at 6 a.m., and for the first time I heard naval guns firing. The concussion was terrific unless you stuffed your ears with cotton. The troops landed an hour later (or at least some people thought that they had and others thought not). The Admiral was trying an experiment to see whether an assault already underway could be postponed an hour. All the landing craft were loaded with troops and in the water on the way to the beach when the signal was out to postpone *H hour* by one hour. There was complete confusion everywhere, and no one knew whether or not to go ahead with the operation. As a matter of fact, some troops landed and some did not and some ships continued firing on the beach and others stopped. It was a perfect lesson in how you can't stop or postpone an amphibious assault once it is underway. There is too much momentum and communications are not good enough. As a result of this experiment, some four or five soldiers were killed by gunfire falling on the beach, which they were not believed to be on.

At 10 a.m., the air raid alarm sounded and I was a bit perturbed to learn that this was not part of the exercise. However, no attack developed and only a little anti-aircraft at very long range was needed to chase away a couple of Hun planes.

The exercise was over that evening, and as we steamed away, the captain was kind enough to invite me to his quarters for dinner. He was delightful and very cordial and I had a very good time. Over port, he toasted Roosevelt and I toasted King George. I remember I made the mistake of rising to my feet, which evidently is never done anymore aboard English ships since some six-footer cracked his head on the beams a century or so before.

I noticed on this and subsequent cruises on British ships that the fighting spirit, among the officers at least, was excellent. They were all keen to get into the fight and come to grips with the enemy, but their equipment on these rather old cruisers, like the one I was on, was very primitive. They had radar to be sure, but because of their lack of experience with it, and the English trait of not accepting new devices, they could not use it effectively for shore bombardment. They worked out their gunnery problems (range and deflection) with the simplest instruments, passed the results by mouth, and trained their guns by hand. They achieved remarkable accuracy in spite of all this.

Back at Plymouth, we took up the job of planning for the great operation ahead. For us in intelligence, this involved sifting through thousands of miscellaneous reports and taking out information pertinent to our sector and evaluating it. One of the greatest problems was to determine the underwater beach gradient, that is to say how gradual the underwater slope of beach to seaward the water's edge was. This was of the greatest importance because it determined how far out our landing craft would ground, especially full of troops and dragging about 4-1/2 feet. It also determined how far soldiers would have to walk through the water under a hail of fire. To start with, the latest available published chart—either English or French—was one based on soundings taken in 1880. The river and the action of the ocean had undoubtedly, completely changed depths and contours since that time. The average tide along our beach was 12-14 feet with a maximum of 20 feet and we knew there was a very gradual slope to the beach. This meant that the water would move in or out by about two or three hundred feet at least. Bob Thayer, in his aggressive way, got permission to go to the Air Force in London where he got their promise to fly several photographic missions along our beach at several stages of the tide. By careful measurements of these pictures, we were able to compute the underwater gradient of beach slope with very considerable accuracy.

Another problem was occasioned by the German employment of underwater obstacles. These were mostly in the form of steel ribs and stakes in various formations (Tetrahedrons and Hedgehogs), which would puncture the bottoms of our landing craft

BEACH OBSTACLES

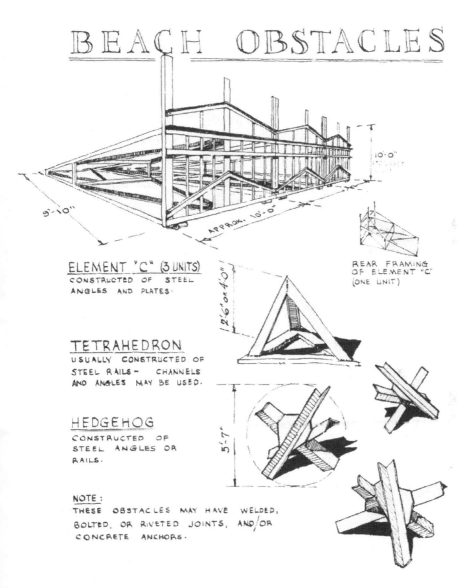

10'-0"

9'-10"

APPROX. 10'-0"

REAR FRAMING
OF ELEMENT "C"
(ONE UNIT)

ELEMENT "C" (3 UNITS)
CONSTRUCTED OF STEEL
ANGLES AND PLATES.

TETRAHEDRON
USUALLY CONSTRUCTED OF
STEEL RAILS - CHANNELS
AND ANGLES MAY BE USED.

12'-6" OR 4'-0"

HEDGEHOG
CONSTRUCTED OF
STEEL ANGLES OR
RAILS.

5'-7"

NOTE:
THESE OBSTACLES MAY HAVE WELDED,
BOLTED, OR RIVETED JOINTS, AND/OR
CONCRETE ANCHORS.

if they ran into them. When we started studying at the end of March of 1944, there were none of these visible from photographs. As the weeks went by, however, the Germans laid out row after row of them until there were five solid rows. The only solution to this problem seemed to be to make the landing at very low tide when all the obstacles would be out of water, and to clear paths through them so boats could land through these clear channels even when the tide was high.

My particular assignment was concerned with the description and location of all other enemy defenses. Most of these were gun batteries and lesser fortifications such as machine gun nests and underground chambers. We received many photographic interpretation reports and also reports originating from the French and other agents in France. All these reports varied quite widely as to the size, type, and particularly the location of the positions. Inasmuch as the positions were heavily camouflaged in most instances, it was of greatest importance to ascertain the exact location of the installations and have them plotted with precise accuracy on our gridded maps so that our ships could fire at them effectively. Harold McGowan and I spent many hours and days together with the Army and Air Force working out precise descriptions and locations. It was essential that all of these branches have complete agreement on the subject. To our astonishment, we found that even two weeks before the operation, several Army branches and the Air Force had only the most fragmentary and confused information on the subject. Bear in mind that here was the greatest operation of all times, a year-and-a-half and more had been spent in planning. Quantities of careful selected personnel were available, and yet this vital information on enemy defenses was not compiled, or even available to the commands that were to carry out the job. To be sure, most of the commands knew some of the important German positions and almost where they were, but none had systematically studied all the latest photographs and reports available, nor compiled the information that seemed to me absolutely essential. Three days before the deadline when operation plans had to be ready for press, Mac and I first discovered that this situation existed. We worked day and night with only four or five hours sleep at night, but we came out with a product that we were both satisfied with. Our information was not only incorporated in our operation plan, but also in those of the Army and Air Force. Our report showed the exact positions of all enemy batteries and strong points in the area. As a matter of record, our entire beach, some twelve miles long, was lined with strong points. Every three hundred yards was a group of machine guns, well embedded and hidden in the sand dunes. There were 19 enemy gun batteries of 45 millimeter caliber or greater, which could bare on ships that were approaching the beach. Most of these guns—there were generally four to a battery—were of large caliber: 150mm, 170mm, and even 210mm.

Let me say a word here about General command assignments. General Eisenhower was in complete charge of everything. British Admiral Ramsay[18] was in overall charge of naval operations, and under him for the American section, Rear Admiral

[18] Sir Bertram Ramsay oversaw the Dunkirk evacuation and the planning and commanding of Naval forces in the 1944 invasion of France. On Jan. 2, 1945 Ramsay was killed as his plane crashed on takeoff near Paris.

Kirk.[19] Under Admiral Kirk there were two task force commanders, Rear Admiral Hall,[20] and ourselves. Each of us was to transport and put ashore one army corp. In our sector, it was the Seventh Corps under Lieutenant General Collins, "Lightning Joe."[21] Admiral Hall was, I think, to land the Fifth Corps, and these two corps composed the Third Army under Lieutenant General Omar Bradley.[22] In each corps there were three or four divisions. The Massachusetts Fourth Division was to be the first to go ashore on our beach which was designated Utah. Hall's beach was Omaha. Brigadier General "Teddy" Roosevelt[23] was in command of infantry in the Forth Division and a colorful figure in all of our discussions. He was to go ashore in the

[19] Admiral Alan Goodrich Kirk was the senior U.S. naval commander during the Normandy landings. After the war, Kirk became a successful diplomat, serving as Ambassador to Belgium, the Soviet Union and Taiwan.

[20] Admiral John Leslie Hall commanded the 11th Amphibious Force in the UK and led the amphibious force "O" which landed and supported the Army V Corps on the Omaha Beach sector off the coast of Normandy. He later commanded the Southern Attack Force during the Okinawa campaign and became commander of Amphibious Force, Pacific Fleet. Eisenhower gave him the nickname "Viking of Assault".

[21] General Joseph "Lightning Joe" Collins earned his nickname during the Guadalcanal campaign against the Japanese. He went to Europe to command the VII Corps in the Allied invasion of Normandy. He later led the Corps to break through the Siegfried Line and played a major role in the Battle of the Bulge. At 47 he was the youngest corps commander in the Army. After the war he became chief of staff to the Army during the Korean War.

[22] After Normandy, Gen. Bradley commanded the Twelfth U.S. Army Group comprising 43 divisions and 1.3 million men, the largest body of soldiers to serve under a single field commander. After the war he headed the Veterans Administration and was appointed the first Chairman of the Joint Chiefs of Staff in 1949. The next year he became the last of nine individuals promoted to General of the Army, a five-star rank.

[23] Brig. Gen. Theodore Roosevelt Jr., son of President Theodore Roosevelt, had a remarkable career before the war, having served as Assistant Secretary of the Navy (like his father and FDR), Governor of Puerto Rico and Governor-General of the Philippines. He had a successful business career as Chairman of American Express and Vice President of Doubleday Books. At 56, he was the oldest man in the D-Day invasion and the only one whose son, Quentin, also landed that day. Tragically, he died of a heart attack about a month after the landing.

first wave with the ground troops he loved. A week before I saw him with tears in his eyes, making a plea at a briefing meeting to support, and in every way possible, save the lives of his men. Lightning Joe Collins was a smart, intelligent figure. He was just like a shot in the arm at any conference. He was on his feet most of the time and came straight to the point. He was often in our intelligence room in headquarters, which Thayer always kept full of the latest dope. All walls were lined with maps and exhibits overlaid with all the latest intelligence. Collins frequently called on Thayer, rather than his own intelligence officer (a very nice but rather ineffective Colonel who was killed three weeks later trying to save his brother in France) for the evaluation of the latest information.

Our own Admiral Moon undoubtedly worked harder than any of them. He was far from stupid, but his mind was a little slow. He had great energy and insisted in knowing everything that his subordinates knew. He never smoked, drank, or had any type of relaxation. I had only two significant contacts with him during this period. The first time, he had gotten word that a daughter had been born in my family and he called me in to congratulate me. The second time he was trying to make a strong case to lay before higher authority for obtaining more ships for his force. He crossed-questioned me minutely regarding enemy defenses and how they compared to the defenses on Hall's beach. The defenses opposing us were almost three times as heavy as on Hall's beach.

It was originally contemplated by the high command in Washington that Moon could be used in the Mediterranean, in connection with Operation Anvil. Anvil was the code name for Combined Allied Assault on the North and South coasts of France, simultaneously. It was subsequently determined (with Eisenhower having the principal say), that our forces were not adequate for this type of operation. Moon was therefore called to England in March to supplement the cross-channel operation. It should be remembered that all the other commands had at least four to eight months more time for planning and preparation.

Life at Plymouth was pretty strenuous. There was no respite from the tremendously heavy work load. We were always very tired and pretty tense. Almost no one got to bed before 1 a.m., and some stayed up every night until 2 or 3 a.m. We were all up at 7 a.m. and at work before 8 a.m. Sunday was no different from any other day. I remember occasionally I would take a jeep just before supper time and tear out to the moors just outside Plymouth. There I would get out and race about the countryside on foot in a desperate effort to keep my balance and avoid becoming over-nervous. Bob Thayer is, and was at the time, a dear friend, but I do not think it was a well-organized office. It was pretty confusing knowing just what one was supposed to do, so one always concerned himself with a little too much. He, however, just loved absolute confusion and was not happy unless there was a three-ring circus going on. For him, it worked because he always had the dope and invariably sold brass hats. However, there just was no organization in our section and it added to my weariness. He had the necessary spark though, and I would do anything for him. The answer was that the work of his section paid off a hundred times over, but it would have been nicer to work under some semblance of organization.

I will never forget the moors just outside Plymouth. I really got to know them very well and they formed the principal alleviation from the terrific pace. They are barren, but they are rolling and lovely, and I hope to take Sis there someday. During the ten weeks before our operation plan was out, I think I took off two Saturday nights for relaxation. The first was to go to a dance, which was a weekly Saturday affair at a former little country club out on the moors. It was not dark until almost 10 p.m. and I spent my first two hours running and walking about the countryside outside the club. When darkness fell, I went inside and stood in a long line to get drinks. It took better than half an hour to get to the head of it. The countryside was very green and the grass closely cropped. The walls between the fields interested me more than anything. They started, I guess, as stone walls, but the earth had drifted in on them and the grass and plants grown over so that they seemed part of the soil itself.

My other Saturday night off was a most successful one. Time and again since, my friends have told me it was the pleasantest occasion they had had out of the States. Late one afternoon in my wanderings to get a little fresh air, I came on a country inn off the beaten path. It was in a lovely spot and I made arrangements with the proprietor for a dinner the following week. The dinner was to be in celebration of my becoming a Lieutenant Commander, and I invited all the fellows in the section, plus a couple of others. It was a splendid occasion, and we had excellent food and wine and a delightful time. All my friends said they had never had such a party. Incidentally, I learned much later that one of the innkeepers daughters continued to correspond for two years with one of my most circumspect friends.

As the weeks went by, our work became even more tense. Everyone looked pretty dull and haggard. There were two more full-scaled dress rehearsals held off the southern coast. I was on a British cruiser each time and I began to learn a bit more about amphibious operations, but hardly enough to be of help to the captain. On one of the exercises, a horrid incident occurred. At about 2 a.m., the general alarm sounded and word was sent out that German E boats were in the area. The E boat was a fast torpedo boat, heavier than ours. Unfortunately, our screen of destroyers was small because two had gone back to Plymouth through a misunderstanding, leaving only three to protect all ships. It was a dark, cloudy night and the E boat darted in, firing their torpedoes at troop-laden LSTs. Two of them immediately blew to pieces, and the third was badly damaged. There were about 1,000 soldiers and sailors in the water, of whom over 700 were killed or drowned that night. Rescue parties seemed slow in finding them. Most were killed by explosions and some at least by the improper method of wearing their life belts. The E boats got away. I believe this was the worst disaster involving water-borne troops during the entire war. I think our Admiral was very much shaken by the incident, though he did not show it.

D-Day was not finally set until a month before. June 5th was finally picked by the high command, partly because the tide had to be low at *H hour* which was to be 6 a.m. Certain other dates, the latter part of May, had also been tentatively selected, but all preparations could not be made to meet them. Our operation plan itself was 500 pages long. It contained all the detailed directions for the 800-900 ships and craft that made up our Task Force 125. I wrote the part of the Intelligence section of the plan that dealt with enemy batteries and gun positions, and also a description of what we knew of some tiny rock islands just off our beach.

To digress a moment, there were two little islands which had been overlooked in our earlier planning and might have been heavily fortified, or at least had observers on them. They were directly in the center of our combat area, and therefore had great tactical value to ourselves and to the enemy. It was our guess that there was no enemy on them, but I strongly recommended that we send a small expedition to them a few hours before the main assault to capture them and use them for spotting our fire and possibly to establish our first shore-based artillery. I requested Bob Thayer to let me go with the expedition to observe and report to the command ship from this central point. He denied me this because I knew too much to risk being captured early in the game. (As it worked out, a small expedition went in as planned, met no opposition, but three quarters of them were killed or wounded from land mines and booby traps).

In the days shortly before the operation, the Intelligence section spent much of its time briefing the different individuals and groups involved. That is to say, we set up graphic exhibits and outlined and discussed their assignments with them. Our naval forces were scattered up and down 80 odd miles of coast and we piled in jeeps with our maps and charts and gave our talks before groups. Of course, at first only the key personnel could be told about the operation. Most of the briefing was conducted in the last few frantic days before sailing, after which all the people who attended the discussion were sealed in their ships and had no contact whatsoever with the shore. Many of the key personnel were briefed in our Intelligence Room where the Admiral used to frequently come himself and bring some of his brass hats. One day I remember the movie actor, Robert Montgomery,[24] and his captain were in. He was the executive officer of a destroyer squadron at that time, and they had just been assigned to our force. Their job was almost a suicidal one because they had to patrol off shore within a mile and provide counter battery fire. As I had pointed out, the Germans had many large caliber coastal defense guns, any of which could have readily sunk a destroyer at that close range. As I described the German shore battery in relation to the positions of the destroyers, the captain started hopping up and down and making grimaces. Montgomery also knew just how tough the situation would be, but he just smiled his whimsical little smile that I had seen often in the movies and settled down to study the situation carefully. This was the second time I had seen him during the war, and I was very favorably impressed. His ship was sunk a few days later off the Normandy coast, but he came through.

The big briefing of the captains of all the ships in the force, as well as of the key army personnel, came about May 29th or 30th. After that, all ships got ready to sail. One of the most interesting sights were the docks and quays all through the southern coast of England. I spent quite a bit of time running about in a jeep and I found every road down to the sea coast was jammed with troops, trucks, guns, tanks, and all other equipment. This was

---

[24] Robert Montgomery was an actor, director and producer. He became president of the Screen Actors Guild in the 1930s and acted in more than 60 films in his career. He joined the Navy after Pearl Harbor and rose to become lieutenant commander. In the 1950s he became an unpaid coach and consultant to President Eisenhower, advising him on his television appearances.

not true of one road, but of all roads for 60 miles within both sides of Plymouth. They were streaming down to the docks and boarding the ships which would load in their turn and then pull out into the harbors to await the word to sail.

Until just about the very last moment, I did not know what ship I was to be on, or exactly what I was to do. Bob determined, however, that his officers should be spread out in different ships and be attached to different activities, so that they would be in good position to report back to the command ship. About three days before sailing, I was assigned to the lead transport with orders to report early June 4th. Those last few days, all that part of England was like a morgue compared to its former activity. All of this section of England was allocated to U.S. camps and maneuvers, and now they were all aboard ship. There were a great quantity of last minute errands to complete, which kept us running about the countryside to a score or more of ports to find a particular ship and give a certain officer last minute instructions. Then on June 3rd, the activity was suddenly over. A few of us were to sail on ships anchored in Torquay Bay, and we met in the afternoon at the Imperial Hotel. It is truly a wonderful spot high on the bluff overlooking the perfect harbor below which was full of ships. We had a good time that evening, and for the first time no responsibilities except to make our ship the next day. It was quite a feeling, no responsibility, nothing we could do for the operation. There was a dance that night in the big ballroom and for the first time it was not stuffed with the U.S. military. We danced and drank champagne until the small hours and after the orchestra left, we entertained the charming singer while she sang and one of our members, "Tommy," who was an excellent pianist, accompanied.

Let me say a word about my feeling about what was ahead. I had, of course, very little time to speculate on that subject. I felt the enormity of the situation, however, and believed strongly that the detailed planning had been superb. It is impossible to overemphasize the importance of planning. Mere force alone does not count materially if you have opposition of consequence. In other words, everyone must know exactly what he has to do under all circumstances that might confront him. Without this, unless the going is easy, you have chaos.

I think as an intelligence officer, I had overestimated the strength of the Germans. Our information was extremely accurate, but it is very easy to overestimate the enemy's ability to utilize his facilities to the fullest. I thought our own naval strength a little weak for the job. As it turned out, we needed every boat we had, and it was like pulling teeth to get what we had. I believe it was an honest commentary to say that the Navy Department hated to spare ships for this operation. Their heart and their ships were in the Pacific, and that was their war and their glory. The Atlantic, and particularly this operation, was an Army problem and a British problem. I therefore felt that we could put the Army ashore, but it was touch-and-go how long we would stay afloat. I had not a moment's fear for my own life, but I did honestly think I would be swimming before I got back. I had made excellent preparations for that. A fine life jacket, a waterproof flashlight, rubber enclosed chocolate bars, and a flask of brandy. After our party, we woke up at 10 a.m. after a sleep in a delightful soft bed. We hurried through breakfast and got a boat to take us to our ships. Everything in the harbor was quiet. All the ships were loaded and ready to weigh anchor. We were the last to get aboard. I was in a long ward cabin with my close friend and associate, Harry Midgely, and about 30 other officers, and a few war correspondents. I was dog tired and tried to sleep that afternoon, but I couldn't. For the first time in my life, I was too tired to sleep. I got almost desperate because I had to have sleep before the operation. I was tight as a drum and my mind was filled with a million details it was too late to do anything about. At 3 p.m. that afternoon, the news spread that the operation was postponed one day. We were to sail in only a few hours, and I know several of the slower convoys must have already left. Well, no one benefited more from that postponement than I, because a kind medical officer gave me a sleeping pill and I was out at 9 p.m. and didn't wake up until 7 a.m. I was a new man and felt like a million. I went right to work after breakfast and worked all that day. In the morning, a large meeting of all the Navy enlisted men was called for me to brief. I discuss with them the parts of the operation in which they were involved. In the afternoon, I worked with army officers and men, describing and discussing Army-Navy coordination measures, and in the evening I had a long session with the Navy commanders. The latter were the naval officers in charge of the ship to shore assault boat movement. I went over and over photos of the shore line with them and discussed land marks, surf, tide, gradients, sand bars, and so forth. It is of greatest importance to have each wave land at precisely the correct spot. I went to bed very happy that night because I thought I had done something.

A word about what went on aboard the ship that evening June 5th. We had onboard the first eight waves that were to land.

Everyone was quiet. No loud conversations. Some men and officers were reading the Bible, all trying to get sleep wherever they
could, most checking and cleaning their weapons for the last time.
There was one air raid alarm about 10 p.m., but the Hun planes
were knocked down without sighting our forces as I learned later.
I had to help one correspondent to light a cigarette because his
hand shook so much that it put out the match every time, no
exaggeration. Messages from Roosevelt, Eisenhower, and others
were broadcast over the loud speaker system, wishing us all well
and giving us their confidence. In the ward room, the executive
officer put up a cut out life-sized picture of his girl in a bath-
ing suit with a comment: *This is what we're fighting for.* Many
of us took exception to it. We were underway at 6 a.m., and
due in the operation area at 2 a.m. It was only 120 miles away.
I remember looking out a port hole at about 10 p.m. There was a
terrific channel current against us and I was sure we were going
only five or six knots. I went to sleep with the feeling that we
would be late.

But we weren't late. I woke up at 1:30 a.m. and went up on
deck. It was cold and the skies dark with heavy broken clouds
blocking out the moonlight. The breeze was fresh and the water
quite rough. At 1:45 a.m., we slackened speed and I knew we
were moving into our position in the transport area. No land, of
course, was in sight because of the darkness. We were ten miles
off shore. I went down and had a delicious breakfast and returned
to my position on the flying bridge. I think it was about 2:30
a.m. when the first activity took place. Searchlight beams and a
blot of anti-aircraft fire went up from the shore and I could see
and hear big explosions. The anti-aircraft fire at times seemed

intense. It looked like waving dotted lines of light against the black. Our medium bombers were dropping their loads along the beach and a little later our heavy bombers, and then again our Thunderbolts and medium bombers. This kept up for two or three hours. At about 3 a.m., our air transports came over. Hundreds and hundreds of C-47s were carrying our parachute troops. They kept coming for about an hour—very low, two or three thousand feet—and I saw them going back empty, after dropping their troops.

Immediately after dropping our anchor, we began unloading troops into the assault boats. This was completed in about 45 minutes and then all their boats milled around in circles in the choppy waters until it was time for them to form into waves and proceed towards the beach. There were 30 troops to each boat and we had 28 boats. They had ten miles to go to the beach and their speed until they got close to shore was six knots. All about us were a lot of dull flashing lights of different colors, which signaled the boats of certain ways to their assembly points, but which could not be seen from shore. At about 5 a.m., our air bombardment off the shore got much heavier and there were flashes all up and down the beach. At 5:10 a.m., the naval bombardment started, and for the first time, the enemy became aware of our presence. It was still very dark and it was a beautiful night indeed to see the white hot shells arching up into the sky in all directions and exploding on the beach.

Shortly before 5 a.m., I had a second big breakfast and then climbed into a small, fast boat, which was to take a ship officer and myself close into the beach to observe and report on the progress of the landings, and for me in particular to report on the degree and type of enemy opposition. The water seemed to be quite rough with five or six foot waves, and I did have sympathy for the poor soldiers who had almost four hours of bobbing around before they set foot on shore. We sped into the beach and were perhaps two thousand yards off shore when the first wave landed. It was light enough to see that distance by then and we could see the first men wading ashore, then moving across the beach to the sand dunes behind. At five minutes before 6 a.m., the gunfire of the ships shifted to the flanks of the assault and inland. At that time, our rocket boats let go their load just before the troops landed. This was a sight to behold. Thousands of five-inch rockets burst all along the shore, and they went off like firecrackers. We could even feel the concussion very distinctly on the water, and one can imagine what happened to the Germans in their dugouts.

As a result of the effective bombardment, there was very little small arms fire on the beach, and I believe that over nine out of every ten of our men got over the beach and onto the sand dunes safely. However, fire did develop from many of the heavier gun positions on the higher ground back of the beaches and on the flanks. A great deal of this fire was directed at the waves of small boats and at the control ships close to the beach. We were going at a fairly rapid speed and had no close calls, but shells were falling very freely in our vicinity. At about 6:30 a.m., one of our ships, a PC, was hit quite near us, and as we closed in to pick up survivors, I recognized a friend of mine who had been skipper, and who I had briefed a few days before. The water was pretty cold, about 56 degrees, and it was necessary to recover the men as rapidly as possible. I remember that this fellow's only concern was that he felt that he had done his best in maneuvering his ship, and hoped the Admiral would not criticize him for having his ship sunk. That feeling was typical. Another casualty we had picked up a little earlier was an Army Captain. He was a tough bird and had been in charge of one of our secret weapons. It was a large Sherman heavy tank that was suspended in the water by a large flotation bag of waterproof fabric. It was propelled through the water by an outward motor at four knots and was barely visible above the water. The idea was that it would approach shore without being observed, and at an eight foot depth, its treads would hit the beach, then discard its water wings, and proceed under its own power. This miracle of a heavy tank suddenly appearing on the beach would scare the life out of the Huns. We had twelve of these tanks on our beach, and ten of them got ashore. On the other American beach, Omaha, they had 20 and only four got ashore. A shell fell close to one of ours and it swamped in about 30 feet of water. An Army Captain and one other escaped after it was on the ocean bottom, but they were well choked up with saltwater. They took it very casually however, and were only sore as hell that they hadn't gotten into the fight ashore.

I spent most of my time trying to spot enemy gunfire, and my knowledge of what guns they had and where located helped a great deal. I sent my reports back to the command ship by radio. Some heavy German fire continued to fall on the beach in and around the water, but it caused no serious trouble as wave after wave landed. The waves kept up for five hours solidly, first landing at 3-minute intervals, then 5 and finally 10. It was by far the greatest build up of troops on shore of all time in any ocean.

At about 10 a.m., we went back to our ship because we had so many survivors on board, and several were in bad need of medical attention. I checked with the captain, gave him my story, and then interrogated all of the survivors they had received during the morning to get a more complete and accurate picture of what had gone on. A few more ships had been sunk than I had realized. I then took a small boat and went back to the *Bayfield*, which was our command ship, and reported to Bob Thayer. I gathered, in spite of the confusion aboard the ship, that everything was going pretty well. So I wrote up my reports, had a big drink, and a good supper.

We stayed off Utah beach for about a month and I shall try to set down a few of the highlights. Our ship was anchored as close to shore as permitted by the depth of water and we could see clearly the activity on the beach and were in constant touch with commands ashore. General Collins,[25] who had been on the *Bayfield*, went ashore the day after the landing. The fifth day after that he assumed full command, relieving Admiral Moon of this responsibility. This indicated that he considered the beachhead entirely secure.

Our casualties were pretty heavy the first week. Over on our beach alone, we took out more than 1,000 wounded each day. This does not include the killed. There was a desperate need for blood plasma. The first few days, until our return convoys to England were properly organized, our ship and every ship was

---

[25] General Joseph "Lightning Joe" Collins earned his nickname during the Guadalcanal campaign against the Japanese. He went to Europe to command the VII Corps in the Allied invasion of Normandy. He later led the Corps to break through the Siegfried Line and played a major role in the Battle of the Bulge. At 47 he was the youngest corps commander in the Army. After the war, he became Chief of Staff to the Army during the Korean War.

littered with wounded. Most of them were on stretchers all through the ship, passages, and every available inch. Many of the original wounded were paratroopers, among whom the casualties had run as high as 60% at the time of their landing.

During these first days, we were also taking out and sending back to England over a thousand prisoners a day. I remember on D-Day I "looked over" a few for intelligence purposes. Many of the rank and file were non-Germans, Poles, white Russians, etc., and a lot of these would talk. However, all of the officers were regular Germans, and they certainly lived up to their reputations of pride and arrogance. They stood up still as ramrods in the boats with their uniforms immaculate in spite of the battle. By their every move and action, they showed that it was merely unfortunate that they had been captured, but it had no great bearing on this battle or the war, which Germany was beyond a doubt winning.

On June 7th, the Navy started to catch it pretty badly. The Germans were masters at devising new types of mines. One of the most gallant jobs was done by our fleet (mostly British) of about 140 minesweepers, which cleared the path ahead of the invasion fleet. However, many of the mines could not be cleared the first day, and in subsequent days these mines cost us many ships. These were magnetic and acoustic mines laid along the shoals of the bay. Sometimes a ship would have to pass over them as many as 15 or 20 times before they went off, and therefore it was next to impossible to sweep them. Also, each night German planes would come over and drop new ones. We lost four or five destroyers to them, two or three larger ships, and many landing craft and ships. Several blew up very close to us. I remember one ST, not 300 yards away, blew into pieces while I was looking at it. It was split in the middle by the huge concussion, and each of the two parts thrown several hundred yards apart. I think there were five survivors out of two or three hundred men on board. Whenever anything moved on the water, it was threatened to be blown to oblivion. All in all, the Navy's losses in this operation were greater than it had been in any previous one, and this was due principally to the mines.

The enemy was not so successful in the air. As a matter of fact, we controlled the air so thoroughly (even from bases in England), that I only saw one German plane in daytime the entire month. However, there were fireworks every night when they came over and bombed the beaches, mined the bay, and tried to hit the ships. They had rather poor luck. For one thing, we were on to their radio-controlled bomb that had been so successful in the Mediterranean. We had radio guards on the frequencies they used to guide these bombs, and when any ship first picked up their use of these frequencies, the code word VERMIN would be broadcast and all ships would jam the frequency. This made it impossible to control the direction of the bomb. The German planes always seemed to put on a lot of pyrotechnics with their raids, and every night at least once or twice, there would be star shells bursting or different colored flames over head. These were principally to guide other planes to their target and may also have been to direct attention. One night, I was rudely awakened about 3 a.m. There was a big noise and the ship shuttered from stem to stem. I got up and dressed very quickly in the dark, thinking we had been hit. Before arriving at my battle station on the bridge, I learned that a very large bomb had missed quite narrowly.

Enemy gunfire on the shore continued heavily several days after the landing. Our ships could temporarily silence most of the guns, but could not destroy them. They would lay low for a while and then suddenly open up. Their fire was aimed at ships close in shore and primarily at the beach where our supply dumps were. I was surprised that the accuracy of these guns was not greater. One day when I was on deck, a gun opened up on a merchant ship a short distance away from us and some 15 and 20 shells fell at about 30-second intervals. Some were over and some were short, but none hit the vessel. (The merchant crew quite reasonably did not like their position and most of them leaped into the water and swam ashore). In as much as enemy batteries were my principal intelligence assignment, I was kept quite busy in trying to ascertain where the fire was coming from. I soon found out that the Germans had a few long-range guns up towards Cherbourg, which they moved about each night. We did know with great accuracy the location of the other guns and could direct ships fire accordingly.

About six days after the first landing, a storm came up which made it impossible to land either men or supplies. A great many of our small craft (used for unloading ships), were tossed high on the beach and were wrecked by the battering of the waves. It was a critical few days because supplies, and especially ammunition, were vitally needed in the tense battle going on ashore. When the storm did not abate on the third day, it was necessary to run several large ships on to the beach at high tide and unload them at low tide. Some of these, or at least parts of them are probably still up there. On the fifth day, the storm did let up and the unloading continued. I happened to be on shore that day and I will never forget the wreckage of boats and supplies that were strewn over every part of the beach. It would have given the enemy great confidence to see it.

My first trip to shore was two or three days after D-Day and I took a jeep up to the site of a great gun battery that had just been captured. Each gun was in a great casement of reinforced concrete, nine to twelve feet thick. I could see occasional pock marks on the walls where our shells had hit, hardly making a dent. Only direct hits in the small mouths could have put these guns out of action. While climbing over the scaffolding of one that was under construction, I heard a noise below of someone moving. I knew none of our troops were in the immediate vicinity, so I filled my pistol and attempted to put a shell in the barrel, but it jammed, so I decided to withdraw hastily. In doing so, I made considerable noise, which evidently scared the person because within a few minutes, two dejected Germans came out and surrendered to my jeep driver. The ever-present and terrifying presence of booby traps was the principal factor that made me more than a little nervous whenever I was on shore. It is difficult to describe the sensation one has when you never know which step you take, or what innocent-appearing object you touch, might cause you to be blown to oblivion. The safe way, of course, was to follow after a mine detector when you were walking and, furthermore, never touching anything. But as an intelligence officer, you could not often do this. I learned somewhat later that some Army intelligence officers had come to the gun battery mentioned above, probably arriving a few hours after me. There were five of them killed because of a concealed trip wire which was connected with a powder storage in one of the encasements.

We were off the coast of Normandy for about a month, until after the Army breakthrough at St. Lo, when it was assumed that our forces had the upper hand and the supplies from England were coming through regularly and smoothly. I was on shore quite a bit off and on during this time, maintaining liaison with the Army and obtaining information of interest to the Admiral. One of the more impressive sights was to see the wreckage left after our airborne troop landing. There were cracked up gliders everywhere and parachutes hung about on trees. Even on the sides of buildings where the paratroopers had been caught. Just as much in evidence around the village of Sainte-Mère-Église were German tanks and other mobile equipment that had been destroyed by our focus on the first day.

The German beach defenses themselves were of great interest to me. Technically, they appeared to be impregnable. Every three hundred yards along the beach there were huge underground fortifications, built of six-to-eight feet reinforced concrete and covered over by sand dunes. The openings were narrow slits and open to cover the beach without direct exposure from the sea. Furthermore, all these underground chambers could be made gas-proof and their doors operated on the same principle as a bank vault door.

I also had the opportunity of seeing one of the launching sites for the V1 rockets. It was a huge great structure of reinforced concrete about 200 yards long by 50 wide. Our air forces had concentrated heavily on these ultra secret sites before D-Day and the anticipation of this new German weapon was one of the important factors which hastened the invasion. These weapons were not used, as I recall, until about ten days after the invasion, but at least we captured some of the launching positions before then.

My happiest recollection of that month was when our ship was steaming full speed back for England. It was the first time that we really relaxed, and I remember just lying on the deck basking in the sun, very grateful to be headed that way.

Back at Plymouth, our thoughts turned to far pleasanter things than war. We were given about four days of freedom and a group of us went off to Torquay for one of the happiest times. There was Harry Midgely, Tom Hughes, Jerry Casey, Bob Mayo and others. We had a grand holiday with squash, walking, golf, dancing, and best of all, just relaxing at the Imperial Hotel. The luxurious feeling of the soft beds and the complete normal atmosphere with no worry in the world was overpowering. We basked in it. On the third day, I had to go up to London to collect what maps and intelligence material I could get regarding our next objective. I spent just two days there, but they were full.

Arriving at Paddington (I think), I was just alighting on the platform when I saw all the people about me throw themselves on the ground. I was motioned to do likewise. In a second, I heard a *chug-chug-chug* high above. Then it stopped. Shortly, there was a tremendous explosion quite nearby. It was my first experience with a Vl rocket which the Germans were sending over at the rate of 15 or 20 a day. Because of this hazard, I was able to get a room quite easily at Claridge's. While I was taking my bath, I heard this thing again and jumped to the window in time to see it going by. It had stubby tail fins and when its rocket motor shut off, it pitched at a sharp angle and exploded probably a half a mile away. I got the full realization then of what the citizens of London were going through with their families, subject to this day and night.

I saw a lot of my friends, including most of those I had been instrumental in sending over. I also called briefly on Mr. William Phillips,[26] and my cousin, Minturn, was kind enough to come in town and we had supper together. I saw Bill Ladd, too, and we compared notes. As soon as I was at least partially successful in getting the information I wanted, I went back to Plymouth, and within a day, we were off for the Mediterranean. The Admiral had flown on ahead with a few of his staff and the rest of us used all of our influence to go by ship, because it meant a ten-day cruise and rest, rather than a mad scramble to start planning another operation. We worked a bit on the way down, getting things together and confirming general information about the new theater war, but also got enough time for sunning ourselves and playing push ball on deck.

---

[26] William Phillips, former ambassador to Belgium, Canada and Italy, was at the time a Special Advisor on European political matters to Gen. Eisenhower. He was from Beverly, Mass., so no doubt knew the Sedgwick family.

The following Top Secret cables analyzing German forces, weapons, and tactics for the August 1944 landings in Southern France will give the reader an idea of the nature of the work Lt. Commander Sedgwick did.

ENEMY FORCES WEAPONS AND TACTICS

PREPARED BY

INTELLIGENCE SECTION (N2)

COMMANDER GROUP 3, 8th AMPHIBIOUS FORCE

ENEMY FORCES, WEAPONS AND TACTICS

The information contained in this pamphlet has been prepared in order that all personnel may have adequate opportunity to become familiar with the characteristics and capabilities of the forces, weapons and defenses of the enemy. At various times the enemy has attempted to use weapons of the kind and in the manner described in this pamphlet. He has rarely succeeded however due to the many counter weapons that have been successfully employed by Allied Forces. A thorough knowledge of what the enemy tries to do will contribute to the success of preventing him from doing it.

The security of this document should be closely guarded. The value of our counter weapons will be impaired if the enemy knows that this information is in our hands.

SECRET

<u>I N D E X</u>

Page

I N D E X

ENEMY AIR

1.   General Appreciation.

    Recently the German Air Force has lost a considerable part of its former sting, and it has not been making itself felt to any appreciable extent against either Allied ground, sea, or air forces. Vast Allied air superiority is perhaps the main reason for the comparitively subdued behavior of the GAF recently, and, in addition, the GAF has been feeling the consequences of the Allied Air Forces' attacks on EUROPE. These attacks have resulted in a decrease of German oil supplies and reserves, curtailment of German aircraft production, disruption of transportation, and the destruction of German planes on the ground and in the air. As a result, the GAF is feeling the depletion of its reserves of fuel and planes at a time when it is called upon to defend against 3 major land assaults on widely separated fronts.

    However, despite our numerical air superiority in this theatre, determined and persistent enemy air attacks against shipping must be expected, especially against exercises and assault areas and against convoys. Although in the NORMANDY operations the German Air Force was singularly ineffectual in attacking shipping, an average of 50 sorties was flown over the area per night, and on one night as many as 175 Long Range Bombers were out. Despite the present rather inactive status of the German Air Force there is a distinct possibility of an all-out determined effort by the GAF anti-shipping units in the MEDITERRANEAN at any time it is considered worth while. Strongest attacks will be made at night (using flares probably); late afternoon and dusk (last light) attacks are a distinct possibility; and dawn (first light) attacks may be attempted. However, surprise attacks by single planes or small groups of planes may occur at any time during the day, and straffing attacks are likely to occur at any hour of the day or night.

2.   Disposition of Enemy Air Force in MEDITERRANEAN as of 12 July 1944.

	LRB	GA	TEF	SEF	RECCE	TOTAL
Italy	(18)	45		70	40	173
S. & SW France	135			30	40	205
Greece, Aegean and Balkans	(10)	70 (50)	60	125(20)	140(40)	405 (120)
• TOTAL	163	115	60	225	220	783

        NOTE: LRB - Long Ranger Bomber, GA-Ground Attack, TEF - Twin Engine Fighter
               SEF - Single Engine Fighter, Recce - Reconnaissance. () Second line
               units

        a. The Enemy Mediterranean Fighter Air Force.

        This Force is already spread thin and is more than occupied by its present commitments.

        b.   The Enemy Mediterranean Bomber Air Force.

        The 135 Long Range Bombers in South and Southwest France are anti-shipping units: JU88 Torpedo Bombers and HE 177 and DO 217 radio-controlled bomb units. These aircraft in S. and SW France comprise about half of the total GAF anti-shipping force. Therefore, these anti-shipping units have been committed to attacking ENGLISH CHANNEL shipping as well as shipping in the Mediterranean.

3.   Tactics.

    a. In general, although the GAF's capacity to launch effective attacks employing the following tactics has been seriously impaired, attacks must be anticipated. Although in the over-all picture their attacks can be expected to be greatly reduced in scale, certain attacks may be very determined and intense.

        (1) All forms of enemy attack (high, medium level, and masthead; glide bombing, dive bombing; radio-controlled bomb attacks; torpedo bombing) are to be anti-cipated. At SALERNO and ANZIO the majority of attacks were low level or shallow glide bombing attacks.

- 1 -   SECRET

The GAF, while varying the altitudes of their attacks, can be expected to make all possible use of terrain screening against radar for their approaches. Approaching from the sea, the aircraft can be expected at any altitude, but low level attacks are the most likely.

(2) Coordinated attacks can be expected at any time and will almost always occur when radio-controlled bombs are being used and will often occur when torpedoes are used.

(3) At ANZIO there were a number of attacks by groups of 40-50 planes. Before coming in for the attack the planes would split up and then come in singly or in small groups from several directions at the same time and at various altitudes, from sea level to 15,000 feet. "Window" (Counter-radar metallic strips dropped from planes) was used extensively by the planes in their approach; and both airborne and ground radar jamming was employed. Certain planes, known as "Spoofers", would fly on the fringe of the area and serve to distract our radars. Until April almost 80% of the bombs dropped were high explosive and 20% anti-personnel; however, with the difficulties the planes were experiencing in getting in to the target proper, the Germans changed to dropping some incendiaries and a higher percentage of anti-personnel bombs, which would be effective in the general area.

(4) Day attacks are not likely in view of allied fighter supremacy and our AA defenses. But, sneak daylight raids may be attempted, in which case the planes can be expected to make all possible use of cloud cover and sun (i.e. attack down sun, and/or out of clouds).

(5) Dawn and early morning attacks proved very costly to the GAF at ANZIO, and these attacks were discontinued. Dusk (last light) attacks came to be expected at ANZIO when (1) there were many ships in the anchorage and there were many Liberty's concentrated and unloading near the shore and (2) a successful reconnaissance had been made earlier in the day.

(6) Night attacks are the most probable. In night attacks torpedo, radio-controlled bombs, ordinary bombs, and mines will be used - any one of these weapons or a combination of any or all of them can be expected. When attacking at night, the planes will most likely approach low over the sea, gaining whatever altitude necessary when they near the target (30-50 miles away), or they will approach overland or behind land masses as far as practicable in order to avoid radar detection.

If there is a moon, the aircraft will approach out of the dark, towards the moon, thus silhouetting the ships against the moonlight.

On dark nights flares will probably be used (although in a recent torpedo attack off NORMANDY no illumination was used). The general tendency of the GAF in illumination and pathfinding in their anti-shipping attacks has been as follows: First, the "Shadower" aircraft sights the convoy or shipping, reports it to the base, and remains in the area outside the range of AA and sends back amplifying reports as necessary. Subsequent aircraft arriving in the area frequently "home" on him. The first element of the Pathfinder force to appear on the scene is the "Turning-Point Marker" if the attacking planes have to go some distance to reach the target or if the target is not easy to find; the Turning-Point Marker drops flares (red, white, green, or yellow) which burn about 20 minutes and indicate to the planes following the turning point for their navigation to the target area. Following the Turning Point Marker the Pathfinder drops a row of float flares to indicate the target, and, if there is considerable cloud cover (up to 6/10), possibly sky-markers in addition. The float flares have most often been the Lux Buoys, electric float lights, usually yellow or white but sometimes red or green; these may blink in a certain pattern, or burn steadily. These markers have been dropped at intervals of from 50-500 yards to 5-10 miles, and they will most likely be dropped at a distance varying from 5-40 miles from the target. They are laid in a predetermined line or lines, and their azimuth indicates either the direction of North, the target, nearest land, etc. The markers having been placed, if illumination is called for, the "Illuminator" planes then proceed to drop illumination flares at 6-9,000 feet in clusters of 5 or 4 at 2 minute intervals over the target area. The most common illumination flares

SECRET

are the pale yellow single-candle or 4-candle parachute flares, which burn a little longer than 5 minutes. According to prisoner of war reports, their ideal illumination for a torpedo attack is a long line of flares laid over the center of a convoy and along its track; the aircraft can then attack diagonally or on the beam and are directly under the flares for a minimum space of time. Red or green flares may be dropped among the illumination flares by the "Master of Ceremonies" plane to indicate whether or not the correct target has been illuminated. If the attack is well coordinated (and they frequently are not), the bombers will then attack.

In approaching the target area the bombers never fly close to the line of Pathfinder flares but keep it just in sight. If the illumination flares are laid off one flank of the ships, the bombers are likely to attack from the opposite flank and head into the flares, in this way they approach from the area of least light and obtain silhouettes of the shipping.

At ANZIO another device for bringing night bombers to their target has been reported: on several occasions 2 shore searchlight beams crossed directly over the port and thereby indicated the target to the attacking planes.

To a certain extent German night bombers can be led to their target by radio directional beams; this, however, has not been found altogether satisfactory, even for their bombing of such large targets as cities in ENGLAND. In the NORMANDY operation the night dive bombers as well as other bomber planes were reported to have attempted to use airborne radar for finding their targets. The German Höhentwiel, airborne radar, has a search lobe of about 18 miles wide. From a height of 160 ft. the plane is reported to be able to pick up a ship's echo up to 25-30 miles. Bomber units in S. FRANCE are being fitted with this equipment.

b. Torpedo Bombing. The torpedo is the enemy's primary anti-shipping weapon. Torpedo attacks may be coordinated with a bombing attack. There have been many instances of coordinated torpedo/radio-controlled bomb attacks; and torpedo mast-head bombing attacks are possible. Usually the secondary attack (bombing) will precede the torpedo bombers. Because of the heavy losses suffered in the past, the German torpedo bomber attacks have recently been staged at night, but dusk attacks are still a possibility. If there is no Moon flares will usually, but not always, be used. In their approach to the target area the torpedo bombers usually apply one of the following procedures:

(1) Fly at sea level to 40-50 miles of the target, climb to several thousand feet altitude, then, when coming within the range of the outer defenses of the target, dive down 2- 3000 ft. to their release altitude of 100-400 ft., and come in.

(2) Fly at sea level until 1 - 2 miles from the target, then climb to 100-300 ft. and release the torpedoes.

The aircraft may vary altitude rapidly for as much as 50 ft. to avoid AA fire in their final approach, but most attacks will come in straight and level. Following the release of the torpedoes (aircraft carrying 2 torpedoes reportedly can, if desired, release both simultaneously, and the torpedoes then follow divergent paths), the planes will utilize full speed, lowest possible altitude, and rapid variation of course and altitude in their withdrawal.

If attacking a convoy, the bombers may parallel the course of the convoy at 12 to 15 miles distance. Usually, when reaching a position 45 degrees from the direction in which the ships are proceeding, they will turn and begin their run-in abreast at low altitude. Torpedoes will be released at distances of from 550 to 2200 yards (usually at the shorter range) and from altitudes from 100 to 400 feet.

German aircraft usually carry 18" torpedoes and have the following torpedo carrying capacity: JU 88 - 2; HE 177 - 4 (reported); HE 111 - 2. The JU 88 is the GAF's principal torpedo bomber, and for some time has been replacing what HE III's still remain in operation. SAVOIA MARCHETTI 79's have been used recently in a few attacks in the MEDITERRANEAN.

- 3 -   SECRET

c. Radio Controlled Bombs. These bombs can be most expected during dawn or dusk and also in night attacks.

(1) The PC-1400 FX type radio corrected bomb is the type most likely to be encountered. It is a 3100 pound armor piercing bomb which resembles a "flying paravane (see sketch, Encl. B). The plane usually attacks across the beam of its target: the bomb is dropped from high altitudes (18- 25,000 feet), falls almost vertically, and is radio controlled only during the last few thousand feet. Its correction is limited to 1600 feet fore and aft and 1100 feet laterally. Like the HS 293, the aft portion of the bomb emits smoke and is likely to show colored lights at night. It is to be anticipated that the weapon will be used only against the largest ships of the force. Turning towards the attacking aircraft and the usual maneuvers used by ships against high level bombing attacks have been employed with good effect. Jamming by ships equipped to do so destroys the radio control of the bomb. FX attacks will frequently be preceded by a low level attack by torpedo planes and/or fighter bombers. Under certain conditions smoke is considered to be an effective countermeasure. There have been reports of a modification to the bomb: namely, the bomb, is connected to the parent aircraft by a thin wire. When the bomb is dropped, the wire is unwound so that the connection between the bomb and the plane remains. Impulses correcting the bombs flight are then sent through the wire to the bomb. This modification, if existent, is an attempt to eliminate the effects of our jamming.

(2) The HS 293 has seen very little use recently, and it is not expected that this type of bomb will be encountered to any great extent in the future. It is an 1100 pound non-armor piercing bomb which resembles and acts like a small aeroplane (see photo, Encl. A). It is about 11 feet long, has a 10½ foot wing spread, and is jet propelled. Flames and a trail of smoke normally follow the bomb, which makes about 350 knots. The HS 293 glider bomb has been used frequently for diversion during simultaneous high level or torpedo bombing attacks. If used, the bombs will be released from a distance of 3 to 5 miles off the ship's port quarter, or starboard bow. The usual altitude of release is 2 - 3,000 feet, but late attacks have been made from 2000 feet and higher. The bomb may approach in a moderate glide to sea level, then come in parallel to the sea, or, approach high and dive vertically. Attacks are normally made from the target ship's port quarter or starboard beam. Two types of approach have been reported: (a) The **parent** aircraft (HE 177, DO 217) -see Encl. (C and D)- comes in on the ship's port quarter, turns as much as 50 degrees, and parallels the ship's course after releasing his bomb. (b) (more likely in night attacks) The plane approaches the target as in a normal bombing run at 3-5000 feet. The bomb is released at 3 to 4 miles, and plane and bomb continue on the same course. At 1 to 2 miles from the ship, the plane turns away and, circling, directs the bomb. In either form of attack the plane keeps its starboard side toward the target since the bombaimer sits in the starboard side of the plane and aims the bomb by lining it up on the target. The parent aircraft must fly straight and level to control the glider bomb's flight, and long range AA, which forces the parent aircraft to take evasive action, is an effective countermeasure. If it is a daylight attack, small caliber AA can effectively engage the bomb itself. Jamming is a standard countermeasure for ships with jamming equipment. Ships should, if possible, turn towards the aircraft in order to present as small a target as possible. Under certain conditions smoke is very effective.

(3) HS 294. This radio controlled bomb is a development from the HS 293. It has not yet been encountered, but reports indicate: It is probably a 4400 lb. bomb. It can be launched from 12,000 ft. or higher during a straight bombing run; the bomb can be launched at a distance so that, by the time the bomb reaches the target, the aircraft is still some 6 miles away and out of gun range. The bomb has jet or rocket propulsion If used at all, this bomb would probably be employed against heavy ships. Jamming, smoke under certain conditions, and the target ship's closing of the range between herself and the parent aircraft will probably be effective counter-measures.

d. High Level Bombing (10-15,000 ft.) by JU 88s or HE 177s should be anticipated at all times. This form of attack may be coordinated with other types of attack, or it may come alone

e. Glide Bombing is most frequently carried out by JU 88s, but Me 410s and FW 190s may also carry out this form of attack. If it is a daylight attack, the glide is usually begun at about 10-12,000 ft. altitude. The dive is shallow, and the bombs are released from 1-2,000 ft. altitude. In night attacks the bombs will usually be released at 3-4,000 ft. or higher. The JU 87 (Stuka) dive bomber can be expected to operate   in night/glide dive bombing attacks when there is a moon.

f. Low Level or Mast-head Bombing by FW 190s principally may be coordinated with a high level bombing or torpedo attack and possibly, straffing attack, or it may come alone. If the mast-head attack is not part of a coordinated attack, the planes will then especially try to cover their run by coming in out of a low sun or out of darkness. In their approach the mast-head bombers can be expected to come in from as many directions as possible and to make all possible use of terrain to screen them from radar; that is, they can be expected to approach from behind hilly terrain, fly over the hills at tree-top level, and come down into the port or anchorage area with full throttle on and at as low an altitude as possible - using the terrain behind them as a screen. During their approach and get-away , the low-level bombers will fly at between 0 and 100 ft. of the water and will release their bombs just before passing over the target ship. The planes will attempt, when possible, to fly between the ships so that the ships cannot open fire without endangering themselves.

g. Composite Aircraft. Recently in the ENGLISH CHANNEL the GAF have introduced a new type of attack which is designed primarily for capital ships or strongly fortified land installations. A ME 109 is mounted on top of a JU 88 (or DO 217), and the composite aircraft flies as a 3-engine biplane under the sole control of the ME 109 pilot. The JU 88 has no crew and is loaded with an estimated warhead of 8,000 lbs; the explosive filling may be as high as 4,000 lbs. About 1 mile from the target and at 2-3000 ft. altitude the ME 109 aims the JU 88, which, still under power and making about 325 mph, proceeds at an angle of descent of about 15° -20° towards the target. After releasing the JU88, the ME 109 dives away in a 90° turn.

So far, this new type of attack has been singularly unsuccessful. Once the JU 88 is released, its course cannot be altered; therefore evasive tactics by the target ship are effective. In order to be successful the JU 88 should be launched from a short distance away, but, if this is attempted, the composite aircraft is exceedingly vulnerable to AA fire and fighter interception.

h. Dive Bombing (by JU87s-Stukas-or JU88s) during daylight hours is the least likely form of attack because of strong allied fighter coverage and AA defenses. The enemy's past daylight dive-bombing attacks were usually carried out at angles of 60° to 80°. The planes make all possible use of cloud cover and sun for their approach and push-over. At times aircraft have circled over-head and maneuvered for position in formation before attacking, and at other times they have broken formation at some distance from the ships and have made individual attacks.

i. Mining. The depths of water in an anchorage or channel will undoubtedly effect the scope of enemy aircraft mining activity. Recently off the beaches of NORMANDY GAF bombers have been principally engaged in this form of activity; the results, such as they are, are more gratifying to them than their recent torpedo and bombing attacks, less danger is incurred by the planes, and no great skill is required of the pilots. Aerial minelaying will usually be attempted at night and in conjunction with another form of air attack which will aim at diverting attention and fire from the minelayers. If the mines are dropped by parachute, the minelaying may be done from altitudes of 2-6,000 ft., but if parachutes are not used, lower altitudes of 500-1,000 ft. will be preferred. On a recent minelaying operation off NORMANDY the pilots were briefed to drop their 2200 lb. parachute mines from an altitude of 2400 ft. The planes flew from their base at a height of 900 ft., then began to climb to 3,000 ft. to cross the French coast, later coming down to 2400 ft. to release the mines. Aerial minelaying can be suspected when there have been over the sea area low flying aircraft which were not observed to attack shipping or beaches. The planes may drop their mines in one run over the area or in a pattern of criss-cross runs some distance outside the range of fire of AA guns. The planes may use radar-jamming equipment and usually use "window" to hinder their being picked up by radar.

SECRET

J. Reconnaissance. Anti-shipping reconnaissance in the MEDITERRANEAN is usually performed by JU 88s, JU 188s, and ME410s; FW 190s can be expected on tactical reconnaissance missions.Over sea areas the reconnaissance is usually conducted at altitudes of 100 to 200 ft. or at 10-30,000 ft. When in search of shipping the reconnaissance planes frequently fly at 100 ft. altitude or below (as low as 15 ft.), and every 15 minutes the pilot climbs to 600 ft., turns on his radar(Hohentwiel), and makes a 360° turn. If any echoes are received, the bearing is noted, and the pilot sets his course towards them with his radar set switched off.

Reconnaissance of ports and inland areas under Allied control is usually performed at high altitudes of 20-30,000 ft.; these port reconnaissance flights are usually performed at night,especially if the ports are well defended -, and night flash-photos are taken. In such instances "Window" is usually dropped in liberal quantities.

4. Air Weapons.

a. Torpedoes: German aircraft torpedoes vary in speed from 33 to 44 and possibly 49 knots; each torpedo, however, is designed to make but one speed. Their range varies from 2,000 to 3300 yds.. The explosive charge is from 400 to 470 pounds of TNT/HND/AI. Depth setting may be adjusted while the aircraft is in flight, and they can vary between 0 and minus 47 feet. Most torpedoes are set to come straight in, but new torpedoes are reported to be capable of being set in flight to vary from 60 to 110 ft. by gyro angling. There are reports of experimentation with a radio-controlled torpedo which is dropped with a radio buoy connected to it by a wire. Signals are then transmitted to the buoy by a parent aircraft, and these signals, retransmitted by the buoy to the torpedo, control the course of the torpedo. The torpedo is reported to leave a green fluorescent wake which enables the parent aircraft to follow its course. The parent aircraft may launch the torpedo at heights up to 13,000 ft. at a distance of 5 miles from the target. There are also reports of experimentation with an electrically controlled torpedo which makes it possible for the pilot to correct the course of the torpedo after it has been launched. However, there are three types of aircraft torpedoes now in use, and these are the ones that are the most likely to be encountered in a torpedo bomber attack:

(1) F 5 B (German); Driven by hot gas motor.
Length: 16 feet. Weight: 1650 pounds. Explosive charge: 550 pounds.
Speed: 33 knots. Range: 3,300 yards. It becomes armed after 220/230 yds., but this arming can be reduced by previous adjustment on the ground. It requires a minimum depth of 50 to 60 ft., and it is usually set for a depth of 11 ft. 6 inches. It is usually dropped from an altitude of 150 feet by JU88s at 187 mph and by HE IIIs at 177 mph. The air rudder usually carries away in the water after staying long enough to prevent the torpedo from rolling while the motor starts and gathers speed.

(2) F 5 W (Italian): Driven by hot gas motor.
Length: 16 feet. Weight: 1980 pounds. Explosive charge:430 pounds.
Speed: 36 knots. Range: Greater than 3300 yards.
It requires a minimum depth of 50 to 60 feet, and it is usually set for a depth of 11 ft. 6 inches. It can be dropped from altitudes up to 328 feet at 187 mph by JU 88s and at 177 mph by HE 111s. The air rudder carries away, taking also the aileron control shaft when the torpedo hits the water. There are no stabilizing fins on the F 5 W. It is considered to be the better torpedo of the two.

NOTE: There is a new electro-magnetic pistol, Pi-SIC, which can be fitted on both the F5W and F5B torpedoes or on a new 21" torpedo. When fitted with this pistol, the torpedo detonates when it comes within 10 ft. of an ordinary ship, and it explodes directly under a ship of average draft breaking the keel. The new 21" aircraft torpedo, to which Pi-SIC can be attached, is reported to have a depth setting of 25 ft. (max. 40 ft.), a max. speed of 42 knots to 2,150 yds., a max. range of 5,500 yds.

(3)LT 350 Circling Torpedo: (Italian)
Length: 8 ft. Diameter: 19½ in. Weight: 840 lbs. Speed: 6 knots at commencement of run dropping to 1 knot over a period of about ½ hr.
Range: Traverses an area 4,920 ft. square (reported).
It is cigar shaped, dark green in color. It has a brass or aluminum propeller and is driven by an electric motor run off batteries. This torpedo is dropped into the water by parachute from altitudes ranging from 6500 to 13,000 ft. The parachute attachment dissolves after being in salt water for approximately ¼ minute. and the parachute sinks.

SECRET

There is no gyroscopic directional control, but a device operated by the motor puts on rudder at intervals during which time the torpedo describes a series of circles of approximately 50 to 80 yds. diameter. When the rudders are freed, the torpedo pursues an erratic course for a few hundred yds. before the device operates again and causes the torpedo to circle. The device incorporates provision for decreasing the amount of rudder each time it operates, and this has the effect of progressively increasing the diameter of the circles. The torpedo reportedly runs awash for about 40 minutes and detonates on impact with a ship or hard surface (but not when it hits the water). .50 cal. and 20mm gunfire can be used effectively against this torpedo. Some circling torpedoes have a self destroying device which acts when the motor runs down; others sink at the end of their run and become magnetic ground mines. Some are reported to remain afloat for several days , only a small part of the warhead being visible; the torpedo remains armed and acts as a sensitive drifting contact mine. The following aircraft can carry 2 LT 350s; (German) JU 88, HE 111, HE 115, DO 217, FW 200; (Italian) SM 79, SM 81, SM 84; the HE 177 reportedly can carry 4.

b. Mines. Aircraft have dropped mines up to 2200 lbs in size. They usually drop ground or moored mines or torpedoes which turn into mines at the end of their runs. Aircraft planted mines have usually been dropped by parachute, but recently off the coast of NORMANDY a great many mines have been dropped without the use of parachutes.

c. Bombs. The radio-controlled bombs Hs 293, HS 294, and FC 1400 FX are discussed in para. 5 above. Inaddition to the incendiary types and to such bombs as the 250 KG (550lbs),500 KG (1100 lbs), 1000 KG (2200), and 2000 KG (4400 lb) of both high explosive and fragmentation types, and the 1400 KG (3100 lb) armor-piercing bomb - all of which have been in use by the Germans for some time -, there are 3 types of small anti-personnel bombs which can be expected: the 250 lb. (Butterfly) bomb with delay action, the BI3E 221b. phosphorous bomb, and the 50 KGSC 110 lb. bomb with delay action up to 2½ minutes. This latter bomb is dropped by parachute. The 3 types can be dropped by planes flying at low levels.

d. Rocket Guns. Fighter and fighter - bomber aircraft may attack landing craft as well as the beaches with rocket guns. However, only a limited number of planes are equipped at present with rockets. Moreover, their effectiveness is limited by the following factors: the fire of these guns is still not accurate, the number of pilots trained to used them is very limited, and allied fighter aircraft opposition will limit their activity.

e. "Window". "Window" is an anti-radar device consisting of metallic strips or silver paper, which is dropped by aircraft in order to set up "blips" which will confuse the radar operators trying to plot the flight. These strips may vary in size, depending on the wave lengths of the radar sets they are attempting to neutralize; some strips have been 3 ft. long, 1 inch wide. The strips can be expected to fall through the air at a rate of 300 ft. per minute. German aircraft have been utilizing "Window" to a liberal extent to cover all types of attacks and reconnaissance flights. When an attack is developing, planes can be expected to drop a heavy screen of "Window" in a crescent-shaped path in the area from which the attacking planes intend to approach. It is especially used by planes (torpedo and reconnaissance) when they begin to climb for altitude in the vicinity of targets.

f. Radar Tail Warning Device. All German bombers and 2 engine reconnaissance planes are now equipped with a warning device, the FuGe 16, which is installed in the tails of the planes and shows the presence of unfriendly fighters approaching them within a distance of 1½ to 2 miles. This device, in forewarning the bombers and reconnaissance planes of the presence of night fighters, enables them to take violent evasive action and thereby elude the night fighters at the last minute. This, or a similar device, has been somewhat successful in enabling enemy planes to escape from our night fighters in several recent night encounters.

g. Pilotless Aircraft. These "Flying Bombs", which have been launched at LONDON from across the CHANNEL, are not expected in this area, but, since it is believed that at least some of them are being launched from mobile sites, there is a bare possibility of their being used in this theatre.

The "Flying Bomb" is a pilotless, mid-wing monoplane with single fin and rudder; the rear portion of the fuselage is surmounted by a jet propulsion unit. The fuselage is 21 ft. 10 in. long, the jet propulsion unit is 11 ft. 3 in. long, and the over all length (including the overhang of the propulsion unit) is 25 ft. 4½ in. long. The diameter of the fuselage is 2 ft. 8¼ in; the diameter of the propulsion unit is 1 ft. 10 3/4 in. The wing span is 16 ft., and the root chord is 4 ft. Apart from the extreme nose of the fuselage and the control surfaces, which are of light metal, the structure is entirely of steel.

The weight of the war head and the blast effect produced are estimated to be comparable with those of the German SB 1000 kg. (2,200 lb) bomb. It is designed to produce maximum blast effect rather than penetration.

In ENGLAND the "Flying Bomb" has operated at an altitude of 1-3,000 ft. and at a speed of about 350 mph. Its range is at least 125 miles. While in flight the track of the "Flying Bomb" is marked by a bright horizontal moving flame and is accompanied by a steady rattling noise similar to a motor cycle engine operating at low speed.

The controls are operated through an automatic pilot monitored by a gyro compass. A clock device is installed to introduce a turn lasting for some pre-determined time, up to 1 minute, at some predetermined time, up to 4 minutes, after the commencement of the flight. An Air-log governs the timing of the flight; at the termination of the flight the controls usually set the "Flying Bomb" into a power dive. Some of the "Flying Bombs" carry radio transmitters which, it is believed, enable the sites to plot the courses of the bombs and make corrections for wind, etc. in the aiming of subsequent bombs. So far, their accuracy is extremely limited, and they can only be aimed to hit within a large area such as the city of LONDON.

The "Flying Bombs" are being intercepted by fighter planes, AA, and balloon barrages.

5. Types of Enemy Planes Most Likely to Be Encountered in the MEDITERRANEAN.

a. Bombers:
JU 88/JU 188-with torpedoes, mines or bombs, at night; reconnaissance by day.

DO 217-with HS 293 or FX bombs, at dusk or night.
HE 177 (in both twin-and four-nacelled versions)-with FX or HS 293 t. bombs, with mines, or with torpedoes, at dusk or night.
JU 87B (Stuka) - Glide bombing and strafing, at night only.
SM 79 (Savoia Marchetti) - with torpedoes, at night.
HE 111 reconnaissance or with torpedoes or mines, at night.
FW 200 (Kurier) - reconnaissance or with FX or HS bombs at night.

b. Fighter Bombers:

FW 190

C. Fighters:

FW 190, ME 109, HE 219(possibly, as defensive fighter with jet propulsion unit.
ME 110 (as night fighter)

d. Reconnaissance:
JU 188, JU 88, ME 410 - long range reconnaissance.
FW 190, ME 109 - tactical reconnaissance.

e. Coastal:

AR 196

- 8 -

6. Types of Friendly Aircraft Most Likely to be encountered in the MEDITERRANEAN:

    a. Heavy Bombers:
        Liberator (B-24), Fortress (B-17), Halifax, (Super Fortress (B-29),
        possibly).

    b. Medium Bombers (twin engine):
        Marauder (B-26), Mitchell (B-25), Boston or Havoc (A-20), Wellington,
        Ventura (PV), Baltimore.

    c. Twin Engine Fighters:

        Lightning (P-38) - by day.
        Beaufighter, Mosquito, Boston (A-20) - as night fighters.

    d. Single Engine Fighters: :
        Spitfire, Mustang (P-51), Thunderbolt (P-47), Hellcat (F6F), Wildcat
        (F4F), Hawk (P-40), Aircobra (P-39), Seafire, Tempest V, (Firefly-
        possibly)

    e. Transports:
        Dakota (C-47, DC-3), Skymaster (C-53), Commando (C-46), Albemarle,
        York.

    f. Coastal:
        Beaufighter, Catalina (PBY), Avenger (TBF), Seafire, Kingfisher(OS2U).

    g. Air Sea Rescue:
        Catalina (PBY), Walrus, Warwick.

    h. Various:
        Piper Cub.

    i. Gliders:
        Horsa, Hamilcar, Hengist, (Hadrian, Waco - CG4A).

ENCLOSURE (C)

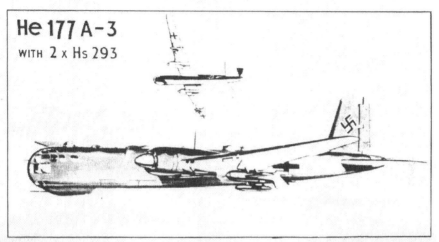

He 177 A-3
WITH 2 x Hs 293

An impression of HE 177 carrying 2 HS 293 (Glider Bombs) below the wing.
HE 177 is also used as a parent aircraft for the FX type radio corrected
bomb.

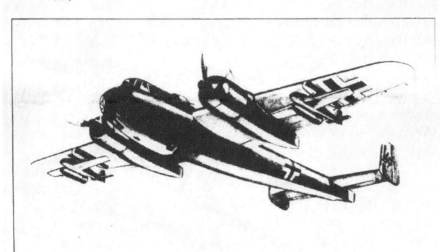

DO 217E carrying 2 HS 293 radio-controlled Glider Bombs. Details of the
installation are unconfirmed. DO 217 is also used as a parent aircraft
for the FX type radio-controlled bomb.

Secret

ENCLOSURE (D)

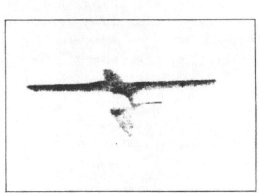

Photograph of the Henschel HS 293
radio-controlled Glider Bomb.

ENCLOSURE (A)

HENSCHEL 293 GLIDER-BOMB

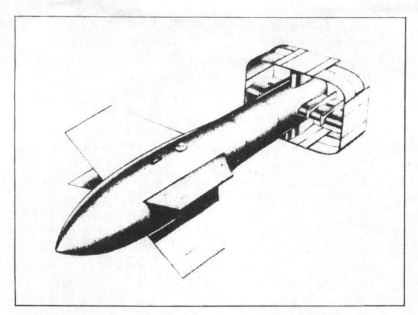

The FX Radio-controlled armour piercing bomb; a provisional sketch.

ENCLOSURE (B)

Secret

ENEMY NAVAL SURFACE FORCES

A. Forces Active in Western Mediterranean.

    1. Heavy Units.

        No enemy heavy units are active in the Mediterranean.
        With respect to the scuttled heavy units of the French and
        Italian Fleets, it has been the policy of enemy to salvage
        the equipment and metal rather than to salvage the unit itself.
        Since the allies have overwhelming sea and air power in the
        Mediterranean, the enemy has been forced to depend upon fast
        light units rather than heavy units both for protection and as
        a striking force.

    2. Light Surface

      a. Active in the Western Mediterranean.

        The following enemy craft are considered active in the Western
        Mediterranean today:

Destroyers	Torpedo Boats	Escort Vessels	MAS Boats	E and R Boats
1	7	12	18-20	12-15

(Continued on following page).

SECRET

(1) Destroyers Italian
(a) The ITALIAN Destroyer DARDO, located at GENOA, has been undergoing repairs. Recently it was moved to an active berth. Length: 315 feet. Standard Displacement: 1206 tons. Speed: 38 knots. Armament: 4-4"7(50), 2-2"5, 2-1.46" AA, 6-21" torpedo tubes, 52 Bollo or 52 Elis or 36 P200 mines.

(b) The ITALIAN Destroyer PREMUDA has been in dockyard at GENOA since August 1943. The latest reports state that its main armament is being remounted.

(2) Torpedo Boats Italian.

ARDITO	GENOA/SPEZIA	Reported scuttled PORTO FERRAJO 10/43. Later reported at GENOA nearly ready 1/44. Presumed active now.
ARTURO	GENOA/SPEZIA	New. Orginally expected ready 7/43. Presumed active now.
AURIGA	GENOA/SPEZIA	New. Originally expected ready 8/43. Presumed ready now.
DRAGONO	GENOA/SPEZIA	New. Originally expected ready 11/43. Presumed ready now.
ERIDANO	GENOA/SPEZIA	New. Originally expected ready 10/43. Presumed ready now.
IMPAVIDO	GENOA/SPEZIA	New. Original report that vessel was scuttled at PORTO FERRAJO 10/43 unconfirmed. Presumed active now.
RIGEL	GENOA/SPEZIA	New, originally expected ready 9/43. Presume active now.

Italian Torpedo Boats are divided into two classes as follows:

ORSA Class   Length: 293 feet. Standard Displacement: 855 tons. Speed: 28 knots. Armament: 3-3.9" (47), 4 17-7" torpedo tubes. Not more thanthree of this class are presumed active.

WAR PARTENOPE
    Class   Length: 267 feet. Standard Displacement: 679 tons. Speed: 34 knots. Armament: 3-3.9", 6 - 1.46" AA Twin mounts 4-17.7" Torpedo tubes, 28 Bollo, or Elia or Harla or 18 P-200 mines.

    Two Torpedo Boats are reported to have been sunk by PT attack 15 June. They were not identified but are believed to be two of the Italian ones mentioned above.

(3) Torpedo Boats French.

BOMBARDE	TOULON/MARSEILLE	This ship has lately undergone repairs, and its armament has been increased. It is presumed ready now.
BALISTE	Believe repairing at TOULON.	
BAYONNAISE	Believed repairing at TOULON.	

    All French Torpedo Boats in the Western Mediterranean belong to the POMONE Class. The specifications of this class follow. Length: 265 feet. Standard Displacement: 610 tons. Speed: 34.5 knots. Armament: 2 - 3.9 " (60) 4 AA mg. 2 - 2.7" torpedo tubes. It is known that the BOMBARDE has increased her armament, and it can be assumed that the BALISTE and the BAYONNAISE will have done so, if and when they become active.

(4) Escort Vessels or Corvettes Italian.

ALCE	GENOA/SPEZIA	Started LEGHORN, fitted out GENOA. Originally expected ready 8/43. Presumed active duty by mid-April'44.
CAMOSCIO	GENOA/SPEZIA	Active at Armistice.
CAPRIOLA	GENOA/SPEZIA	New. Originally expected ready 9/43. Presumed active since early '44.
CICOGNA	GENOA/SPEZIA	Active at Armistice.

-11-

MARANGONE	GENOA/SPEZIA	Now Originally expected ready 9/43. Presumed active by mid-April '44.
RENNA	GENOA/SPEZIA	New. Originally expected ready 9/43. Started LEGHORN moved to GENOA 1/26/44 for fitting out. Presumed active since mid-April '44.
TUFFETTO	GENOA/SPEZIA	New. Originally expected ready 8/43. Presumed activ since early '44.
VESPA	GENOA/SPEZIA	Active at Armistice.

Two corvettes previously reported refitting at SPEZIA have been reported active at GENOA. These are probably PERSEFONO and EUTERPE, previously scuttled and refloated at SPEZIA.

Two corvettes were engaged off VADA ROCKS by Allied forces May 23/44. One was sunk, the other damaged. They were identified as Numbers 2222, and 2223 of 22 UJ Flotilla. It has been reported, and reconnaisance tends to confirm in large part, that there were at that time eight corvettes of the 22UJ Flotilla and that their numbers ran from 2220 to 2227 inclusive. Others were reported building and some nearing completion.

One UJ boat, 800 tons was reported sunk off CIOTAT June 10 by an Allied submarine, and another probably sunk off Cape Sicie June 9 by the same submarine.

With four corvettes reported put of of action and two returned to active service, it is estimated that 6 Italian Corvettes are active.

STROLAGA and ARDEA have been fitting out for some time at GENOA and should be ready soon. DAINO is fitting out at GENOA having been removed from LEGHORN 1/26/44 CORVO fitting out in LEGHORN was believed to have been damaged January '44 in an air raid. Present status unknown.

The reported specifications of the Italian corvettes follow, but must be treated with some reservation until confirmation is received. Length: 210 feet to 240 feet. Tonnage: 5/600 tons (possibly up to 800 T). Speed: 25/30 knots (25 is probly more nearly correct). Armament: 1 - 37 mm twin mount on after deck, 2 20 mm quads fully automatic, one on bow, one of after deck slightly raised above 37 mm, 1 - 100 mm Capprel on forecastle, old Italian make hand loading and ramming, 4 DC throwers and 2 DC racks, 2 rocket projectors ahead of each DC rack. Space was allowed for torpedo tubes and on each side of vessel just aft of the stack, but the were not installed and Breda Guns (20MM) have been mounted in their stead.

(5) Escort Vessels French.

AMIRAL SENES	TOULON/MARSEILLE	New Construction from Port du Bouc.
ALICE ROBERT	TOULON/MARSEILLE	Converted banana carrier.
CURIEUSE	TOULON/MARSEILLE	Reported scuttled TOULON 11/42. Refloated and repairs begun 7/43. Presumed active now.
DEDAIGNEUSE	TOULON/ MARSEILLE	Reported scuttled TOULON 11/42. Refloated and repairs begun 7/43. Presumed active now.
IMPETUEUSE	TOULON/ MARSEILLE	Reported scuttled TOULON 11/42. Refloated and repairs begun 7/43. Presumed active now.
RAGEOT de la TOUCHE	TOULON/MARSEILLE	Completed late '43. Active.
ENSEIGNE V BALLANDE		Believed near completion at Port du Bouc

(6) Miscellaneous Anti-Sub Vessels.

Miscellaneous Anti-sub vessels of the 22nd UJ Flotilla include two Auxiliary Escort vessels, over 225 ft.; 2 SC's 190 ft.; 1 newly completed KT vessel specially armed for escort duty; and a number of converted Trawlers and Yachts.

(6) (cont'd)

The Germans have also made wide use of the following type Landing craft and it may be expected that they will be encountered in an landing operation in the Mediterranean.

German Tank Landing Craft - These craft were designed and built for the invasion of England. Subsequently they were modified and adapted for use as mine and net layers, flak boats, gun boats, and escort ships for coastal convoys. Some of these craft have been fitted with wide shelves on either beam to carry mines (LCT (II).

Since 1940 the Germans have built up to 300 LCTs. Construction ceased almost entirely in 1943, but has recently been resumed. Thirty-three(33) are at present under construction. The majority of these craft are at present in the Channel and North Sea area, but many are in the Mediterranean.

German units have been trained in the use of smoke screen, flame throwers, and small torpedoes which are to fired from landing barges in case of an invasion.

TYPE	LENGTH	BEAM	SPEED	ARMAMENT
IA	156'	21'	7-12	1-2.9"; 1 or 2 m.g.
IB	156'	21'	7-12	1-2.9": 2 - 1 1.46": 1 or 2 m.g.
IIA	156'	28'	7-12	1-2.9": 1 or 2 m.g.
IIB	156'	28'	7-12	1-2.9": 2-1.46": 1 or 2 m.g.
III	160'	21'	7-12	2-3.5": 2 or 3-1.46": 0 or 1-0.79"
III	156'	21'	7-12	2-3.5": 2 or 3-1.45": 0 or 1-0.79"

Pointed
Bow

| IV | 165' | 21' | 7-12 | 1-3.5": or 1-2.9": 1 or 2 m.g. |

German Siebel Ferries - With minor variants, a Siebel Ferry consists of two powered barges serving as pontoons for a bridge or deck which unites them side by side with considerable space between the sides. They have two functions: (1) mobile, flak, river gun boats, or mobile coast defense artillery; and (2) ferries and lighters for troops and vehicles, accomodating as many as 150 men at a time. The Siebel Ferry is well known for its African and Mediterranean operations. These crude pontoon rafts support formidable fire power on a small and mobile target. They constitute an excellent platform for surface or AA gunnery in sheltered waters, and may be used especially in positions inaccessable to naval batteries.

Length	Beam	Speed	Armament
80'	50'	8-10 knots	3-3.47"; 2-1.46"

(7) E. Boats
The Seventh Flotilla of 12-15 E.-boats is at the present time operational in the Mediterranean theatre.

Tactics of E-Boats.
The following tactics were employed by E-boats in the English Channel.

E-Boats are small fast aggressive vessels which carry torpedoes and operate in a manner similar to U.S. PT Boats against convoys and individual ships. They are difficult to pick up on Radar and have managed to slip through screening patrols and launch successful torpedo attacks against LSTs and other landing craft. It is probable that at night E-boats and U-boats acting as "torpedo boats" on the surface will present the greatest surface threat to our Convoys. For this reason an understanding of the tactics employed by these craft and the best known means of defense against them is of primary importance.

E-boats normally attack during darkness. Attacks on Convoys be expected any time after dark and withing one hour or two of daylight. They start out in a flotilla of approximately ten and break up into groups of three or four boats which spread themselves over a ten-mile area and cruise at about five knots searching for shipping. They approach usually from broad on the seaward

-13-

bow of the van of the convoy. Attacks on the landward side are not unknown as on several occasions E-boats have passed through the Convoy while escaping.

Attack is usually made after the first escort vessel of the Convoy has passed the last group of the E-Boats. E- Boats. choose their targets individually, and fire their torpedoes at full speed (38) knots. The normal range is about 1100 yards but they have been known to use as short a range as 600 yards. They fire their torpedoes singly and the torpedoes have a range of 6,500 yards. After firing their torpedoes they make a 180 degree turn to get out of the range of defending guns and retire in order to reload their torpedo tubes. This action normally takes no longer than 5 minutes.

The new type of E-Boats carry both mines and torpedoes . They also sometimes use a form of depth charge to attack pursuers. Mine laying E-Boats try to avoid, convoys. They usually operate in groups of three laying a row of mines in the war channel after establishing their position by means of the buoys. A sharp "crack" from the small sounding charges they use just prior to laying has occasionally been heard under ideal conditions. Boats carrying both mines and torpedoes attempt to lay mines unobserved and then lie in wait for a convoy possibly in a different part of the channel and attack it with torpedoes. E-Boats use various expedients to meet counter-measures employed by escorts. For example:

(a) They take cover behind or close to a light buoy or wreck.
(b) They take position or steer parallel to the route down moon from the convoy.
(c) When pursued, they double back with the aid of smoke and attack the convoy from the rear. On one occasion an E-Boat attacked from the bow and passed through the Convoy, but it is usually the policy to avoid becoming engaged.
(d) Sometimes attacks are delivered independently by groups of three, sometimes by larger numbers. On one occasion as many as 15 were encountered.

E-Boats depend upon their speed for defense and retire quickly after their presence is disclosed. They use smoke effectively and extensively. Sometimes they double back and attack through their own smoke. They have been known to drop smoke floats to simulate a damaged boat while the layer makes a sharp turn and breaks away . They are particularly disconcerted by illumination, and they do not like aircraft. When retiring they make straight for home over shoals to avoid pursuit if possible. Direct co-operation between E-boats and aircraft has recently been attempted by the Germans. Aircraft dropped flares, apparently in order to silhouette the Convoy and facilitate attack by E-Boats.

E-Boats can operate in seas of up to Force Five. Smooth seas are preferred for minelaying sorties, but torpedo attack can be carried out in rough weather. No operations are normally carried out for five or six days before or after the full moon.

 Characteristics of E-Boats. - There are three types of E-Boats in use by the Germans. Type A and B are used in Norwegian, Baltic and Mediterranean waters. Type C are the newest and largest E-Boats and are operating in the English Channel, North Sea and a few in the Mediterranean. The following information is relative to types B and C:

TYPE B
Displacement: 86 tons (full load)
Lenght: 106 feet
Horsepower: 3,600
Speed: 34.5 knots (max)
Endurance: 500 miles at 30 knots, 600 miles at 22 knots.

Type C
Displacement: 95 tons
Lenght: 106 feet
Breadth: 16 feet 6 inches
Draught: 5 feet 6 inches
Double wooden hull.
Armor protection: None except for arm ored bridge with plating between 0.59
          and 0.79 inches thick.
Main Engines: Three Diesels (H.P. each engine 2000 at 1630 revs.)
Rudders: Originally fitted with one, but the use of three has re-
          cently reported. Steering is direct.
Exhausts: Not fitted with silencers and are discharged underwater.
Speed: Cruising, 31 knots, maximum, 38 knots, dead slow 12-15
                       knots. Speeds of less than 12 knots may be obtained by
                       the use of one engine.
Guns: One(1) 20 mm in a well in theforecastle and one(1) 20 mm
                       on stand aft. Rate of fire 480 r.p.m. It is thought
                       that a 40 mm. in now being fitted to replace one (1) 20 mm
                       aft in some boats. Twin and single machine guns, hand
                       grenades, rifles and bayonets are also carried.
Torpedo tubes: Two (2)
Torpedoes: Torpedoes 4x21" air torpedoes; Two (2) of which are in the
                       tubes, and two (2) are spares.
Mines: E-Boats may be used to lay various types of mines. An E-
                       boats will never carry a full compl ement of mines, torpedoes
                       and depth charges; a combination, for example of six (6)
                       mines and torpedoes (in tubes) is however possible.
Depth Charges   Six (6) Three on each side aft on mine rails, when no
                       mines are carried. E-Boats usually carry only buoyant
                       depth charges.
Searchlights: One (1) fitted to mast.
Smoke C nisters: When working properly a smoke screen can be made for ½ hours.
                       In addition smoke buoys are carried.
Scuttling Charges: Twelve (12) usually carried.
Radar: There are indications that about two (2) in each flotilla
                       are being fitted with aircraft type Radar with a range of
                       approximately 3 to 4 miles.
Seagoing Complement: One (1) officer, about three (3) chief and/or petty
                       officers and twenty (20) men.

    (8) MAS Boats Italian

    MAS Boats of 110 ft. have a speed of 35 knots, Those of 50 ft. to
70 ft. have a speed of 45 knots.

    MAS Boats are a combination of our own PT and PC Boats. They are
armed with two (2) torpedoes (type W-200), one (1) 20 mm machine gun and with
depth charges containing 80 kilograms of explosives. (MSA 502 carries two
(2) torpedoes, type A-100, and a 13.2 Breda Machine Gun). All MAS Boats have
inter-ship radios and a few have long range radios to keep in communication
with their base. MAS Boats were designed originally for hit and run tactics,
but are now used extensively for convoy escort.

    B. Considered Active in A.riatic

    (1) Destroyers - No destroyers are considered active in this area
at the present time. PIGAFETTA is having her main armament remounted
and possibly may be ready soon.

    (2) Torpedo Boats
AUDAGE   TRIESTE /POLA/FIUME.   Active at Armistice. Old and believed
                                        used chiefly for mine laying.
DEZZA   TRIESTE/POLA/FIUME.   Active at Armistice.
GLADIO   TRIESTE/POLA/FIUME.   New. Originally expected ready 8/43. Com-
                                        pleted at TRIESTE since 11/43.
INSIDIOSO   TRIESTE/POLA/FIUME   Active at Armistice.
MISSORI   TRIESTE/POLA/FIUME.   Active at Armistice.
STELLA POLARE   TRIESTE/POLA/FIUME   New. Originally expected ready 7/43. Com
                                        pleted at FIUME 12-43.

115-FT. E-BOAT TRAVELLING AT HIGH SPEED.

GERMAN "E" BOAT: TYPE "C"

ENCLOSURE (A)

Secret

ENEMY SUBMARINES

1. Availability and Disposition.

The Germans are believed to have about 400 submarines of all types, some 300 of which are operational. About 200 of the latter group are of the 500 ton and 740 ton classes. The known concentrations of submarines are as follows:

(a) BAY OF BISCAY - One hundred thrity (130) 500 ton and 740 ton U-boats were concentrated here prior to the NORMANDY invasion. It was reliably reported that 50 of them were being held in reserve to oppose that invasion, and it would appear from reports of activity in the CHANNEL and its Western Approaches, that at least 50 had been assigned to that function. However, the remainder of the BISCAY fleet apparently is not so engaged.

(b) NORWAY - Reports prior to NORMANDY invasion indicated 40 submarines were based in this area.

(c) BALTIC - Numerous reserve, experimental, obsolete and partially trained U-boats are based in the BALTIC, some of which could be called out in emergencies.

(d) MEDITERRANEAN - Nine (9) 500 ton U-boats are based at TOULON and 1 or 2 are based in the ADRIATIC. Also 3 submarines are reported fitting out at SPEZIA.

2. Details and Characteristics of Enemy Submarines.

(a) Characteristics of Common Types.

Type	Length	Beam	Draught	Speed	Armament
250 ton	136½'	20'	12½'	1*77	3-21" torpedo tubes; 1-0.79" AA gun.
500 ton	206' to 220'	20'	13'	15.5/8	5-21" torpedo tubes; 1-3.5" gun; 1-0.79" AA gun (recently some refitted with 2 single mount and 1 quadruple mount 0.79" AA and no 3.5" guns).
740 ton	244½'	20½'	13½'	18.5/8	Six (6) 21" torpedo tubes. 1-4.1" gun 2-0.79" AA guns (recently some refitted with 2 single mount and 1 quadruple mount 0.79" AA gun and no 4.1" gun).
1200 ton	280'	26'	16'	18-20/8	6-21" torpedo tubes; 1-4.1" gun, 1-0.79" AA gun (larger guns may have been replaced by more AA armament).

In addition to the above the Germans have some 1600 ton minelaying and supply submarines and a few large submarines captured from other nations.

(b) Prefabricated Submarines. Recently all construction on 500 ton and 740 ton submarines has been halted in favor of a new U-boat whose hull is assembled from 6 prefabricated sections. The assembly period is only 6 weeks. One such hull, 245 Ft. in length and 17 to 18 feet in beam is known to have been launched. Other details are unknown. This may be the submarine which is reported to have 2 pressure hulls with oil between and to be capable of diving to 1300 feet.

(c) Midget Submarines and Human Torpedoes.
(1) "W" Boat - Reported small German submarine capable of 35 knots surfaced and 25 knots submerged. It is about 90 feet long and wide beamed. The conning tower, which is the only part visible at normal trim, is 13 to 17 feet long, 5½ feet wide, 6 feet high and very streamlined in appearance. Two torpedoes are carried in tubes forward; spares are not carried. The failure of this craft

-17-

to appear during the NORMANDY invasion casts doubt upon its
operational existence.

(2) Other Midget Submarines - It has been reported that the enemy
is building large numbers of small submarines, whose hulls are
assembled from six prefabricated sections. The specifications
are:

Tonnage - 180 tons
Length - 73ft.8in.
Beam - 11ft.5in.
Draught - 17ft.2in.
Surface Speed - 12 knots.
Maximum Diving Depth - 700 ft. (approx.).
Crew - 12
Torpedoes - 16 (normal caliber).

It is believed that some of these submarines may be sent by rail
to TOULON for operation in the MEDITERRANEAN. In addition, wide
experimentation with midget submarines has been observed in the
BALTIC SEA and one type, known as HELA II, has been built in
some quantity. It is 96 feet long and 12 feet in beam; its
other characteristics are presently unknown. Also the enemy
possesses a few ITALIAN four-man submarines, which, however, have
not been particularly successful in operation.

(3) Human Torpedoes, Explosive Boats, etc. - "Neger" or German One-
Man Torpedo. A unit consisting of 2 standard 21" electric
torpedoes secured one above the other. The operator sits under
a transparent dome in the upper (or mother) torpedo in the space
normally occupied by the war-head and releases the lower (or
child) torpedo when within range of the target. The unit is
launched from the shore, and has a speed of 3½ knots, with an
endurance of 12 to 15 hours. The "child", which proceeds as a
normal torpedo after it is released, has a speed of 20 knots and
a range of 2000 yards. At least 36 units were launched at ANZIO
without any finding a target. In NORMANDY their use was again
reported without any considerable success. However, it is
possible that an improved or modified form of this torpedo may
be encountered.

Two-Man Italian Torpedo - A 21" torpedo, 22 feet long, war-head
500 pounds, speed 2½ knots, endurance 12 to 15 miles, normal
depth 12 to 15 feet, with maximum of 50 feet. The torpedo is
operated by 2 men in shallow diving gear who set astride it and
attach the war-head to the target ship. Italians have used it
with considerable success.

Explosive Boat - An 18 foot speed boat capable of 35 to 40 knots,
explosive charge about 770 pounds. The driver arms the charge
500 yards from the target, and escapes on a folding raft.

Two-Man Torpedo Boat - A 22 foot boat capable of 34 knots,
endurance 100 miles, torpedo carried aboard. The boat is aimed
at the target and the torpedo is dropped stern first at a range
of 9000 feet or less.

Radio Controlled Boats and Torpedoes - The enemy is reportedly
experimenting with radio-controlled motor torpedo boats capable
of launching one torpedo, radio-controlled flat bottomed boats
containing high explosive charges and various sized radio-controlled torpedoes. Apparently, all are designed for use against
invasion vessels.

(d) New Technical Developments in Enemy Submarines. Important new developments have been made in the torpedoes carried by enemy submarines.
Practically all such torpedoes are electrically propelled and almost
half are equipped with acoustic homing devices. It is believed that
the acoustic homing torpedo is set to run on a straight course for
a distance equal to the distance from the submarine to the point
where the torpedo should collide with the target. If no hit is

-18-

scored within this pre-set run, the acoustic gear takes over and homes
the torpedo on the sound of the ship's propellers. Also torpedoes
which will circle or execute zigzag courses have been employed.

New equipment installed on submarines includes anti-aircraft
rocket projectors and super-sensitive, multiple hydrophones with ranges
of 15 to 20 miles, and an accuracy within one degree. Some 740 ton
and 1200 ton submarines are reported to be equipped with helicopters
for observation purposes. These helicopters are towed on a cable 250
to 300 yards long, and land and take off from the platform just aft
of the bridge. Another new development is "Schnorkel" which is an
extensible diesel air inlet and exhaust, enabling submarines to proceed at periscope depth at about six knots using their diesel motors,
and to charge their batteries while at that depth. Anti-detection
devices include: German G.S.R., which gives warning of enemy use of
radar; radar decoy balloons anchored to floats with tinfoil hanging
from the balloon to give false radar targets; radar decoy spars
mounted in buoys with tinfoil attached to give false radar targets;
and SBT (submarine bubble targets) which are chemical pills that
create large under-water disturbances and give false asdic targets.

3. Enemy Submarine Operations in the Mediterranean.

During the month of May enemy U-boats made four attacks in the Western
Mediterranean, torpedoing one destroyer and 3 merchant vessels, only
one of which sank. After each attack Allied vessels and aircraft
hunted down and sank the attacking U-boats. This reduced to 10 the
number of submarines operating in the Western Mediterranean and since
that time there have been no attacks or sign of activity by the remaining U-boats. All of these U-boats are based at TOULON. One was later
destroyed by air raid on TOULON.

A heavy anti-submarine screen is maintained at the STRAITS OF GIB-
RALTAR to prevent the entrance of U-boats into the Mediterranean. However, it is estimated that, in the event the BISCAY bases are captured
by Allied Armies, the U-boats based in BISCAY might attempt to run this
screen in order to reach the base at TOULON. Outside of this possibility
it appears unlikely that the number of ordinary sized U-boats in the
Mediterranean will be materially increased. However, midget submarines
may be shipped by rail to TOULON, or other enemy ports for use in this
area.

4. Enemy Submarine Tactics. No new offensive tactics have been observed in
this area. In evasive maneuvers, enemy U-boats are submerging deeper
and deeper. In a recent "kill" in this area the U-boat submerged over
600 feet, and in the ATLANTIC, one submerged to about 850 feet. Another
maneuver is to bottom the U-boat in considerable depths thereby decreasing the chance of detection by Asdic. Of course, the standard
tactics of evasive turns are used as well as the anti-detection devices
mentioned in section 2 (d).

UNDERWATER OBSTACLES

A. Ceneral Information.
    Underwater obstacles have been used extensively by the enemy in defending beaches
from amphibious assaults. Boaches like those in northern France where there is an
appreciable rise and fall of tide present an area of beach below high water where many
obstacles can be placed in a complicated net work of defenses. Beaches in the Mediterranean where there is very little tide can not be expected to be defended in exactly the same manner. For instance in Normandy all obstacles at low tide were above the
water line. In the Mediterranean obstacles can be expected to be continuously underwater. The description which follows of the type of obstacles and the know German employment of this form of defense in the Normandy invasion is however indicative of the
general pattern that the enemy can be expected to employ.

    Each day the enemy is improving his defenses and may be expected to alter and add
to them right up to D-day. Therefore, a knowledge of his methods is important. It is
expected that the enemy will make full use of the equipment and techniques already
developed and make every effort to obstruct the approaches to all beaches considered
possible for use in a large scale landing.

B. Anticipated Results from Use of Obstacles.
    The enemy when first placing obstacles on a beach does so in order to hinder a
landing thereby giving him more time to bring the attacking elements under fire and to
organize his defenses for the attack. As additional obstacles are placed in position,
the purpose shifts to that of actual destruction of the implements of the attack in the
water or on the beach. This shift is accomplished by increasing the number of obstacles to be encountered and by attaching various lethal devices to them.

C. Types of Obstacles.
    The placing of obstacles on the beach and in the water is under the immediate
control of the local Army Commander of the enemy. The obstructions used and methods
of placing the obstructions vary with each locality and depend on the material available.

    Sketches of three (3) main types of obstacles used by the enemy are shown below.
Of those shown,   the hedgehog, and tetrahedron are most frequently used,
and Element C is used the least, probably because of the quantity of material required
in its construction. The obstacles have usually been made of steel but have recently
appeared in cement or wood. Various adaptations are often noted such as a concrete
base for a steel hedgehog. This serves the dual purpose of anchoring the obstacles
and of raising its height. The enemy has also used jetted rails (sharpened railroad
track) placed in the sand at such an angle that it will pierce the bow of small boats
attempting to land. Wooden stakes, the size of telephone poles, barbed wire, and
cement posts or blocks have also been observed.

D. The Position of Obstacles.
    The area in which underwater obstacles are effective is limited by the tidal
range and the gradient of the beach. The tops of the obstacles must be within 3 or 4
feet of the surface of the water in order to be effective. Thus, where a slight tidal
range is coupled with a relatively steep gradient, the area which is available for the
placing of obstacles is limited. In an area of this type relatively effective placing
of obstacles may be accomplished in a short period of time with less material. On the
other hand, in an area of shallow gradient and large tidal range, such as the Normandy
Coast, a very extensive area must be covered in order for this type of defense to be
fully effective.

E. Priorities in Placing Obstacles on Beaches.
    The enemy uses obstacles to strengthen the already existing strongpoints and to
force the landing craft into the fields of fire of its batteries. Thus, if there is a
"blind spot" in a strongpoint it is strengthened by means of obstacles in an attempt to
force landing craft away from it into the arcs of fire of the guns of one or more
strongpoints.

F. Mining of Underwater Obstacles.
    In an attempt to destroy the landing craft in the water the enemy has attached
mines to the underwater obstacles. Specially prepared "T" or Tellermines, "S" or anti-
personnel mines and captured shells have been utilized for this purpose. The "T"
mines are attached to any and all types of obstacles in such a fashion that the detonation of them would be lethal to small landing craft on contact. The "S" mines are
attached to poles rising several feet above the water and are linked together by a

-20-   SECRET

wire or cable. A tug on the wire detonates the mine which has a far reaching lateral effect. The enemy visualizes the use of such a mine field as having the same effect as artillery fire.

G. Sympathetic Detonation of Mines on Underwater Obstacles.

Considerable difficulty has been encountered by the enemy with underwater mines because sympathetic detonations frequently destroy the mine fields they have established. They are not able to place the mines on every obstacle because of the likelihood of one detonating another. The movable pressure cover of the "T" mines has an extensive surface which heretofore has been the governing factor of detonation. This cover is now being removed and the means of detonation modified so that "T" mines can be placed about 30 feet apart. Covers have also been designed for shells and "T" mines which protect them from the influence of the sea water and reduce the possibilities of an underwater transmission. This allows more concentration of mines on a beach and more nearly approaches the enemy's goal of one mine per meter of obstacles.

H. A Typical Arrangement of Underwater Obstacles.

In preparing to defend a beach with underwater obstacles the enemy first places hedgehogs, or tetrahedra at the halfway mark of the area to be defended by obstacles. In a tidal area obstacles are located so that they constitute a hazard from mid-tide to high water. In a non-tidal area the obstacles will probably be first located with their tops just below or on the surface of the water. The work from the halfway mark is continuous so that when one row of obstacles covers the entire beach another row is started usually to seaward of the original. Thus a typical arrangement would include from two to three offset rows of hedgehogs and tetrahedra. When the rows to seaward are completed, work is started landward from the original row. The distance between rows and between the individual obstacles will vary depending upon the size and importance of the area to be defended. The obstacles probably will not form a complete barrier but most often will allow passage of a small boat if properly marked channels are established.

After the hedgehogs and tetrahedra are in place, a general intensifying program is undertaken. This usually consists of placing several rows of stakes to seaward and between the existing rows of obstacles. Thus the field of obstacles is not only intensified but expanded to seaward.

The beach strongpoints are the first to be fronted by obstacles and this area is usually more extensively fortified than other areas. Element "C" is often used to strengthen the seaward defenses of the strongpoints. When this work is well underway an engineering unit places the various types of mines on the obstacles. They too at first follow a skeleton pattern and subsequently are increased as supplies of mines, labor and time permit.

Ultimately, the size and importance of the area to be defended, the amount of material available, and the amount of time in which the enemy can work, will determine the density and types of obstacles on a beach. There is no perfect pattern and only by increasing the number of obstacles in the area can the defenses be improved.

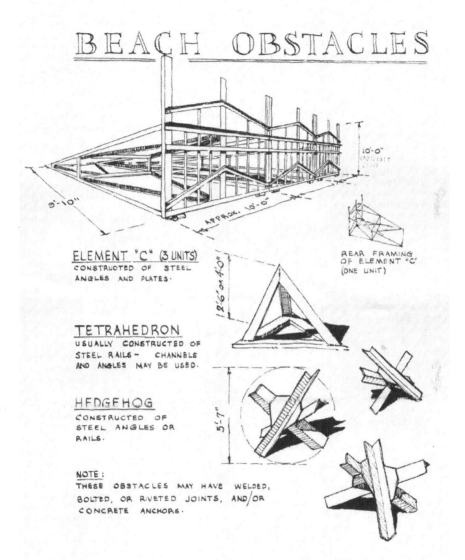

ELEMENT "C" (3 UNITS)
CONSTRUCTED OF STEEL
ANGLES AND PLATES.

TETRAHEDRON
USUALLY CONSTRUCTED OF
STEEL RAILS — CHANNELS
AND ANGLES MAY BE USED.

HEDGEHOG
CONSTRUCTED OF
STEEL ANGLES OR
RAILS.

NOTE:
THESE OBSTACLES MAY HAVE WELDED,
BOLTED, OR RIVETED JOINTS, AND/OR
CONCRETE ANCHORS.

REAR FRAMING
OF ELEMENT "C"
(ONE UNIT)

SECRET

MINOR BEACH DEFENSES

1.   The minor beach defenses which may be encountered along enemy coastal areas suitable for Allied landings consist of the following:

(a) Infantry positions.
     (1) Blockhouses (casemates, pillboxes and fortified buildings).
     (2) Strongpoints (permanent positions usually containing groups of pillboxes, machine guns, trenches, ditches, barbed wire, mines and possibly anti-tank guns.
     (3) Fire trenches and weapon pits.
     (4) Anti-tank gun positions.
     (5) Machine gun positions.
     (6) Mortar positions (see "Enemy Coastal Batteries" in this pamphlet).

(b) Coast Artillery positions. (see "Enemy Coastal Batteries" in this pamphlet).

     (1) Anti-aircraft gun positions.
     (2) Dual purpose gun positions.

(Continued on next page.)

(c) <u>Field Artillery positions.</u> (see "<u>Enemy Coastal Batteries</u>") in this pamphlet

    (1) Field Gun positions.
(d) <u>Engineer installations.</u>
      (1) <u>Anti-tank Obstacles and Roadblocks.</u>
        a. Chevaux de frise. (Hedgehogs and X-shaped rails, inter-strung with barbed wire.)
        b. Steel or iron rails.
        c. Cement cubes, pyramids, cones, stakes and tetrahedra; Hedgehogs and Element "C" (see "<u>Beach and Underwater Obstacles</u>" in this pamphlet).
        d. Ditches extending along beaches.
        e. Cement walls extending along beaches.
      (2) <u>Barbed wire along beaches.</u>
      (3) <u>Minefields.</u>
        a. Anti-tank mines.
        b. Anti-personnel mines.
      (4) <u>Demolitions.</u>
        a. Mined bridges and roads.
        b. Mined buildings.

2. Casemates, pillboxes, and fortified buildings located in advantageous positions are observed and reported throughout all coastal regions. These defenses are found in port areas, along the beaches or immediately behind them, along railroads and highways, or at important intersections where they are often associated with roadblocks. Almost all of these defenses are camouflaged as garages, villas, fishermons' cottages, beach houses or any other structure to blend in with the surroundings. Whenever possible, according to reports, houses have been transformed into casemates and pillboxes, but otherwise new structures have been erected. It is reported that every house and villa along the beaches has been converted into some type of blockhouse and for all practical purposes any building along the beaches should be considered to be fortified.

3. In general, casemates differ from pillboxes only in size and in the calibre of the guns found in them. Casemates vary in size from 25 feet to 50 feet in length and width, while pillboxes vary from 25 feet to 6 feet in length and width. Both are similar in shape, being designed to offer no plane surface to fire. The walls of the casemates are reported to be of concrete, in many cases not reinforced, and vary in thickness from 6 feet to 13 feet in the front and 3 feet in the rear, while the walls of the pillboxes probably vary from 3 feet to 1 foot in thickness.

4. According to reports, the casemates contain guns up to 88 mm., while the pillboxes probably have nothing above heavy machine guns.

5. Anti-tank obstacles, consisting of walls, ditches and concrete blocks, are observed and reported along many beaches.

6. Roadblocks are also noted along many beaches and are of several types: Cement walls, cement cubes, iron rails and chevaux de frise (hedgehogs and X-shaped rails interstrung with barbed wire).

7. Both anti-tank obstacles and roadblocks are similar in appearance and construction to underwater and beach obstacles, illustrations of which may be found in this pamphlet on PP.

8. Barbed wire is observed along almost every beach. It is located in front of Anti-tank ditches or anti-tank walls where they occur.

9. Minefields, containing anti-tank mines and anti-personnel mines are observed and reported along several beaches as well as in some inland areas directly behind the beaches.

10. The following sketches are illustrative of typical minor beach defenses found along enemy coastal areas:

-23-

A SECTION OF GERM

THIS PANORAMIC SKETCH IS INTENDED TO FAMILIARIZE PLANNERS
ACTUALLY ENCOUNTERED ON A TYPICAL SECTION OF THE ENEMY C
PHOTOGRAPHS OF A SIMILAR AREA ARE SHOWN. OTHER OBSTRUCTION
ENEMY BUT NOT SHOWN ON THIS SKETCH ARE:

CD BATTERY   BOOBY TRAPS   ANTI-TANK WAL
RR GUNS   MINED BUILDINGS, ROADS, AND BRIDGES   CHEVAUX DE FF
ARMORED TRAIN   ANTI-TANK AND ANTI-PERSONNEL MINES   HEDGE HOGS
MOBILE ARTILLERY   SHALLOW WATER AND DEEP WATER MINES   IRON AND STEE
FLAME THROWERS   NETS AND BOOMS   STEEL RAILS IN
CASEMATES   ROAD BLOCKS   BELGIAN ELEME

INDEX TO DEFENSES ON SKETCH:

1 — 105 MM (DP) GUN EMPLACEMENT   6 — AMMUNITION STORAGE   10 — BARBED WIRE
2 — COMMAND POST FOR DP BATTERY   7 — L A A EMPLACEMENT   11 — MG EMPLACEMENT
3 — SOUND DETECTION POST FOR DP BATTERY 8 — FIRE TRENCH   12 — SEARCHLIGHT EMPLACEMENT
4 — RANGE FINDER FOR DP BATTERY   9 — 3 MG WITH CONNECTING COMMUNICATION TRENCH AND CENTRAL CONTROL, 13 — ANTI-TANK DITCH
5 — PREDICTOR FOR DP BATTERY   SURROUNDED BY SEVERAL STRANDS OF BARBED WIRE 14 — CONCRETE PILLBOX

FENDED COAST

RSONNEL WITH DEFENSES WHICH WOULD AT THIS DATE BE
REALISM ONLY THOSE DEFENSES CONFIRMED BY AERIAL
WHICH ARE FREQUENTLY FOUND TO BE EMPLOYED BY THE

KNIFE RESTS
VARIOUS TYPES AND DESIGNS OF BARBED WIRE
CONCRETE· CUBES, PYRAMIDS, CONES, TETRAHEDRA, AND DRAGON'S TEETH

CONFIDENTIAL

BEACH, MINED
PROBABLY FORTIFIED BUILDINGS AND WALL
FORTIFIED BUILDING
CO OR HOWITZER EMPLACEMENTS
OUNDED BY WIRE

20 — WALL, POSSIBLY DUMP
21 — WALLED DUMP WITH 2 HUTS
22 — FREYA RADAR
23 — 3 FLAK TOWERS, DUAL MOUNT AA
24 — HUTS

25 — RR ON EMBANKMENT
26 — COASTAL ROAD
27 — LANDING BEACH

PREPARED BY N-2 SECTION, COMNAVNAW
MARCH 20, 1944

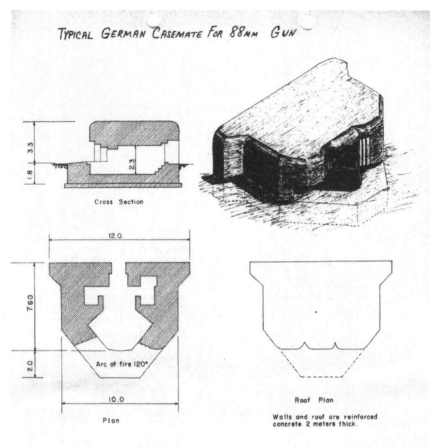

TYPICAL GERMAN CASEMATE FOR 88mm GUN

Cross Section

12.0

7.60

2.0

Arc of fire 120°

10.0

Plan

Roof Plan

Walls and roof are reinforced
concrete 2 meters thick.

(DIMENSIONS ARE IN METERS)

COASTAL BATTERIES

1. <u>General Remarks</u>: The German plan for defense from attack by sea places great dependence on coastal batteries. For example the whole coast of France is 1200 miles in length and best estimates early in 1944 reveal that there were over 2000 guns of 88 mm. calibre or larger employed as static coast artillery. This is an average of 1.7 guns per mile. The coasts of other German occupied countries are similarly defended.

The system of coastal batteries is designed by the Navy although largely manned by the Army. The Navy controls the elaborate warning system as well as all defenses until the assault force lands; then command except for Naval installations at once reverts to the Army. The Army and Navy chains of command are therefore dovetailed: both are almost invariably based on the major ports. The location of coastal batteries has been primarily in accordance with the following three principles:

    a. For the protection of ports and harbors
    b. To bring maximum possible fire power to bear on and off the potential landing
        beaches.
    c. So as not to be subject to capture by a surprise landing.

Concentration of batteries are therefore noted about the larger ports while there are long stretches of rugged coast with few if any positions. In the vicinity of beaches coast defense guns of relatively heavy calibre are sited on the headlands and entrances to the gulfs and bays and on the high ground ½ to 2 miles behind the beaches. In this manner not only the beaches themselves but the approaches to them and the inland exits can be enfiladed with heavy fire. In addition batteries of lighter guns are placed on small promontories at the ends of many beaches in such a manner as to bring cross fire directly on the beaches.

In areas where the inland terrain is mountainous or rugged the enemy has prepared many positions which do not contain guns but which do provide all the necessary facilities so that mobile artillery may be brought in and set up on short notice when the direction of the attack has been determined. This work of preparing positions in advance has not been found as necessary where the inland terrain is more level and guns may be set up in any open field with only minor preparations.

2. <u>Types of Guns.</u>
The Germans have used captured enemy equipment to the maximum extent possible. This is especially true of the heavier (over 170 mm.) coast defense guns. As a result they employ a wide variety of types and calibres which tends to complicate the problem of supplying ammunition and training gun crews. Furthermore most of the guns are not of recent make or design and are not readily adaptable for use with modern fire control equipment. Fire from most batteries is controlled by visual methods and pointing and training of individual guns is done by hand. Radar constitutes the main element in the warning system and is occasionally used to control the fire of certain German made guns such as 88 mm. batteries. It can be said that on the basis of experience to date the accuracy of their fire has not been outstanding in comparison with that of our own Naval gunfire and it has proved more harrassing than destructive.

Probably 90% of all coast defense guns are mobile and can be readily moved from their fixed positions on short notice. It is quite common practice therefore that when a battery is threatened with air or Naval bombardment which it can not effectively answer the guns will be moved to a hiding place or to another temporary position. Permanently fixed targets for Naval gunfire are therefore not to be expected in most instances.

The following table lists the probable predominant calibre of guns used by the Germans together with their estimated maximum ranges.

CALIBRE	MAXIMUM RANGE	REMARKS
75 mm. (2.9")	18,000 yds.	
88 mm. (3.46")	22,000 yds.	Dual purpose
105 mm. (4.14")	13,000 yds.	Howitzer
105 mm. (4.14")	19,000 yds.	
138 mm. (5.41")	18,000 yds.	
149 mm. (5.90")	20,000 yds.	
150 mm. (5.91")	14,000 yds.	Howitzer

-24-

150 mm. (5.91")	25,000 yds.	
152 mm. (6.00")	22,000 yds.	
155 mm. (6.1")	14,000 yds.	Howitzer
155 mm. (6.1")	26,000 yds.	
170 mm. (6.7")	32,000 yds.	
220 mm. (8.7")	25,000 yds.	French Naval Guns
240 mm. (9.4")	40,000 yds.	

It should be noted that the ranges given are taken from artillery tables and are not to be considered as distances at which any degree of accuracy can be obtained. Experience has shown that one half to two thirds of these ranges are more reasonable estimates for effective firing.

3.   Description of Individual Batteries (See sketches) A typical static coastal artillery position consists of 4 or 6 gun emplacements laid out in the shape of an arc or V. The spacing depends on the size of the guns and the contours of the land. Near the center of the formation is an observation post which is generally also used as command post. To the rear are underground shelters, magazines, and living quarters. Range and height finders are located in appropriate spots nearby and an elaborate system of communications including personnel trenches connects all the individual positions. There are also direct wire, and sometimes teletype communications, with nearest radar and aerological stations. The battery also includes 6 or 8 light AA guns and occasionally 2 or 4 88 mm. dual purpose guns. On the outskirts of the area there are machine gun positions and it is commonly surrounded by barbed wire, an anti-tank ditch and minefields, all to protect against ground attacks. The entire battery might cover an area 250 yards in width by 150 yards in depth. A 4 gun medium battery would require about 250 troops including infantry to man ground defenses.

The Germans take full advantage of camouflage and also often place dummy positions resembling the real battery several hundred yards away.

4.   Protection for Guns. Over the last 6 to 9 months especially, the Germans have been concerned with the protection of their coast defense guns from air and Naval bombardment. On parts of the Invasion Coast many guns are now housed in reinforced concrete shelters or casements. (See sketches). Some of these have roofs up to 12 feet thick and walls of 16 feet. They are almost invulnerable to everything but direct hits in the opening for the gun barrels. They ordinarily require some 6 to 9 months to construct and large quantities of material and labor. At present therefore the program has only progressed to where selected batteries along the more vulnerable sections of the coast are enclosed and in the other sections only certain occasional batteries have their guns in casements. Most frequently in the Mediterranean Theatre guns are in open circular emplacements having a cement foundation and protected on the sides by sand bags or earth revetments. In some instances walls of blocks of stone have been erected.

DETAILS OF TYPICAL BATTERY

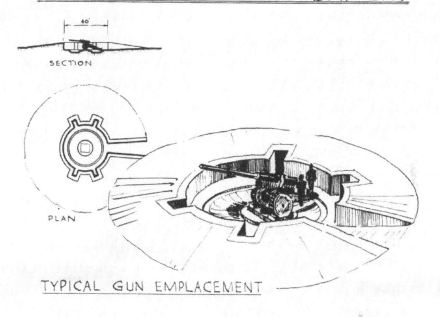

SECTION

PLAN

TYPICAL GUN EMPLACEMENT

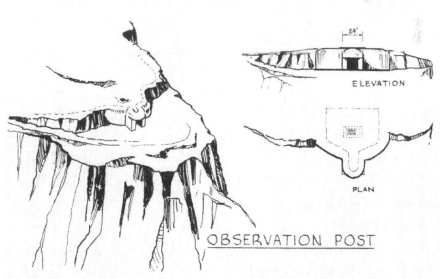

ELEVATION

PLAN

OBSERVATION POST

TYPICAL GUN EMPLACEMENTS

TURRET MOUNT, 240-280 MM

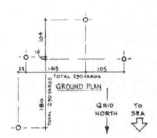

CASEMATE, 105-150 MM

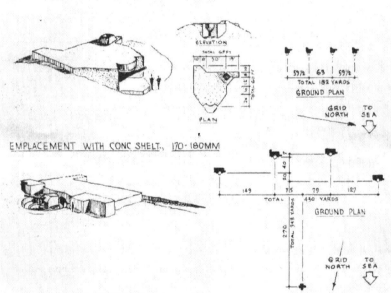

EMPLACEMENT WITH CONC SHELT., 170-180MM

OPEN, 155 MM HOWITZER

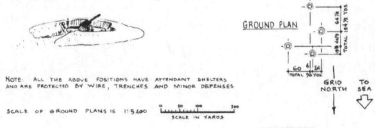

NOTE: ALL THE ABOVE POSITIONS HAVE ATTENDANT SHELTERS AND ARE PROTECTED BY WIRE, TRENCHES AND MINOR DEFENSES

SCALE OF GROUND PLANS IS 1:5400

SCALE IN YARDS

MARINE MINES

The following brief description of marine mines is of an informative nature only. It by no means covers the subject and is in no way intended to modify any manuals or instructions or to be interpreted as a directive on counter-measures.

From the beginning of the war the enemy has displayed considerable energy and ingenuity in the development of new types of mines and in the adapting of existing types to meet special conditions. The enemy may be expected not only to have already planted mine fields in the assault areas out to the 300 fathom curve, but he may also be expected to supplement these by night planting of mines using: (1) aircraft, (2) E-boats, and (3) smallcraft.

During Operation NEPTUNE the enemy planted numerous mines at night by planes. These were, for the most part ground mines and were usually planted either in already swept channels or in areas that were congested with anchored Allied shipping.

The enemy employed the following tactics:(1)Marker flares outside the transport areas were often laid by the enemy before the planting of the mines, (2) The enemy would send a few bombers to drop bombs in conjunction with the mining operation. Mines from planes were sometimes dropped from low levels and at other times parachuted from high altitudes using black weighted parachutes.

The existing types of mines which may be expected are:
1. Ground Mines.
   Ground mines may be expected in waters varying in depths from 2½ to 30 fathoms. These are of the following known types:
   a. Magnetic
   b. Acoustic
   c. Magnetic-Acoustic Combination
   d. Pressure-Acoustic and/or Magnetic Combination.

All of the above types may have time delay clocks or special devices, which will delay detonation until a given number of ships have passed over them ("clicks"), which delay arming of mines up to an 80 day period). However, unless the enemy anticipates not only the locality of our assault but also the approximate time, it is not believed that time delay clocks will be used. Clocks set for short delay periods in mines planted during an operation may be expected. German mines have been discovered which were not actuated until 15 "clicks" had been run off, but experience has shown that 6 is the maximum number of "clicks" normally expected.

The Pressure-Acoustic and/or Magnetic mine (Oyster Mine) operates on a new principle of non-contact firing. During Operation NEPTUNE the pressure mechanism was introduced in "GG" mines in combination with an acoustic unit. It could also be used in a "GC" mine in combination with a magnetic unit. It could also be used in a "GC" or "GO" with a magnetic and an acoustic unit.

Since the danger of this mine increases with the size and speed of the ship and the shallowness of the water, there are few theaters of operation where Oyster mines would be effective.
2. Drifting Mines.
   Drifting Mines, can be planted in any depth of water. These are of the following known types:
   a. Contact
      (1) Sea Battery
      (2) Chemical Horn.
      (3) Contact.
   b. Snag Line
   c. Magnetic

These are the least expected type of mines. This is due, in large measure, to the fact that there are few definitely predictable currents in the Mediterranean, and to the fact, that they are normally the most difficult type to lay with any degree of effectiveness. These are most liable to be contact, sea-battery type equipped with an antenna of copper wire up to 80' long.

3. Moored Mines.
   Moored mines can be planted in water from 5 to 500 fathoms deep. However, they are seldom planted in over 200 fathoms of water. These are of the following known types:
   a. Contact
      (1) Sea Battery
      (2) Chemical Horn
      (3) Contact

SECRET

b. Snag Line
c. Magnetic

In localities where there is no appreciable tide rise and little current the moored mines would be the most used of any type of already planted enemy mines. Without the problems of tides and currents this type of mine is not liable to move along the ocean's floor, and, therefore, will not present a hazard to the enemy's shipping. Also these mines take less critical materials, and their use is much more flexible than any other type.

4. Controlled Mines.
Controlled Mines are most often found at river mouths and entrances to important harbors, in depths from 2 to 300 fathoms. These mines are controlled from a shore station and cannot be swept; they have to be destroyed by counter-mining.

5. Torpedo Mines.
a. Circling.
b. Straight-running.
The Germans have on several occasions used the Italian circling torpedoes against Amphibious Operations and against crowded harbors. These normally turn into ground-magnetic mines or drifting contact and have been very difficult to sweep due to the congestion in the area.

Recent convincing evidence has been found of the existence of German 21" torpedoes, which run to a predetermined range then become a ground mine. They can be fixed either by submarines or E-boats, probably are electric, with a maximum range of 3 miles. They are trackless, carry about 600 pounds of explosive charge and are probably magnetically activated.

Anti-Sweeping Devices

In any moored mine field various types of anti-sweeping devices may be found. The number and type of these is absolutely unpredictable.

One type consists of an anchor with a streamlined conical, aluminum alloy float which is about three feet high and one foot three inches across at the base. This supports an explosive charge and a firing mechanism, which is hydrostatically controlled.

If the obstructor is cut and has risen to the surface, it should then be armed.

Generally, when sweep wires contact the mooring cable they are brought up to the firing mechanism. Then, when thirty pounds of pressure is exerted, a small charge of TNT explodes severing the sweep wire.

A second type of obstructor or anti-sweeping device is a knife blade cutter on a swivel suspended from an empty mine case.

Another type is explosive cutters suspended from floats or shackled into a mine mooring cable.

Anti-sweeping devices are usually within mine fields. However, they are sometimes found outside the field. The presence of these devices may be detected by:
(1) A small underwater explosion,
(2) A clean cut in a parted sweep wire, or
(3) Sighting of mine floats.

Sabotage

For sabotage purposes the enemy (particularly the Italians) in the past has made considerable use of several types of mines. Some of these are designed to be attached to the hulls of ships in port. Since some of the Italian experts in this field are known to be working with the Germans, it is possible that some of the following types might be encountered:

1. Limpet Mines.
The charge in this type mine is carried in a metal container inside an inflated rubber ring which holds it against the ship's bottom. The mine is fired by a time clock unless it becomes detached from the ship, at which time it rises to the surface, and is fired hydrostatically.

2. Barnacle Mines.
These mines are attached to the bilge keel of the ship with several C-clamps. This mine is armed and detonated by the forward motion of the ship. Normally this mine is in an elliptical casing.

3. Ring Mines.
These have about eleven to thirteen pounds of explosive charge and are attached to the hull of a ship by suction. They are either about twelve or fifteen inches in diameter.

-27-

CHEMICAL WARFARE CAPABILITIES OF THE ENEMY

1. Chemicals and Chemical Weapons Available to the Enemy.
   a. GENERAL. The enemy is well prepared to employ chemicals against future operations should he elect to do so. He has good chemical resources, munitions and weapons. His troops and airforce are well trained in chemical warfare. Aside from the nitrogen mustards, which are well known to the Allied Forces, it is probable that no new gases of importance have been developed by the Germans, but improvement is expected in methods and concentration of employment and in mixtures of known agents.

   b. PARTICULAR TYPES OF CHEMICALS AND CHEMICAL WEAPONS AVAILABLE TO THE ENEMY. The following is a summary of the particular types of chemicals and chemical weapons which may be available to the enemy.
   '(1) Blister Gases (mustard, nitrogen mustard, lewisite, "arsenical oil", crude phenyldichlorarsine, and mixtures of these which may be dispensed by:
       (a) Bulk contamination vehicle (sprinkler carts);
       (b) Chemical mines on the beaches;
       (c) Smoke Howitzer shells;
       (d) Rocket bombs for smoke mortars;
       (e) Aircraft bombs with fuze impact or air burst;
       (f) Airplane spray; probably low level and not above 1,000 feet;
       (g) Vesicant-oil mixtures on the water just off the beaches;

   (2) Choking or Lethal Gases (phosgene, diphosgene, Chloropicrin, hydrogen cyanide, cyanogen chloride, etc., and mixtures of these which may be dispensed by:
       (a) Howitzer shells;
       (b) Rocket bombs for smoke mortars;
       (c) Aircraft bombs;
       (d) Anti-tank grenades;
       (e) Floats or submerged tanks off the beaches;

   (3) Teargas (chloracetophenone, brombenzyl cyanide, etc., and mixtures of these, which may be dispensed by:
       (a) Any weapon firing HE;
       (b) Generators;
       (c) Anti-tank or anti-pillbox grenades;
       (d) Floats or submerged tanks off the beaches;

   (4) Nose Gases (Adamsite, diphenychlorarsine, etc., which may be dispensed by thermogenerators which have been handplaced, dropped from planes, or inserted in water floats or submerged tanks off the beaches.

2. Types of Gas Attacks Available to the Enemy Against Amphibious Operations.
   a. ATTACKS AGAINST PERSONNEL ON OFF SHORE SHIPS. Personnel on off shore ships which are not close in shore are less vulnerable to attacks from chemicals, but the following types must be considered possible:
   (1) Armor-piercing shells from shore batteries may carry a proportion of irritant agents mixed with HE.
   (2) Aircraft bombs charged with blister gas;
   (3) If there is a moderate off shore wind with no fog or rain, large concentrations of choking, lethal or nose gases released from land installations or offshore floats or submerged tanks could be in casualty producing quantities 10 to 15 miles off shore.
   b. ATTACKS AGAINST PERSONNEL IN LANDING CRAFT APPROACHING THE BEACH. If the enemy elects to employ gas, the first important chemical attack on the landing force may be directed against personnel in landing craft approaching the beach. He may estimate that an attack at this time would cause great confusion and, in forcing the wearing of gas masks, would render the actual landing more difficult. Troops in landing craft are subject to the following types of gas attack:

S E C R E T

CHEMICAL WARFARE CAPABILITIES OF THE ENEMY (Cont.)

(1) Blister gases from aircraft bombs with fuzed airburst at 100 to 300 feet altitude;

(2) Low-level airplane spray (under 1,000 feet) with blister gas liquid, probably from intruder type planes;

(3) HE with 10% tear gas to harass personnel and force the wearing of masks;

(4) Nose gases from generators on the beaches or water floats;

(5) Choking or lethal gases from rockets, particularly if there is an off shore breeze and no rain or fog.

c. ATTACKS AGAINST PERSONNEL WADING ASHORE. Personnel wading ashore must be prepared to meet all of the chemicals likely to be encountered while in the landing craft approaching the beaches. In addition, the enemy may place on the surface of the water, by means of floats, submerged tanks, or rockets, a mixture of 10% mustard and 90% fuel oil. Such a film on the last 50 yards to the beaches would constitute a definite chemical hazard to those having to wade ashore.

d. ATTACKS AGAINST PERSONNEL ON BEACHES AND INLAND. If the enemy decides to use chemicals against future amphibious operations, it is probable that he will make full use of all available chemicals and chemical weapons on the beaches and inland thus enabling him to hold ground with a small number of men until the arrival of reinforcements. Once chemical warfare has started, high HE charge in chemical shells may be used, and therefore all loud explosions upwind must be treated with suspicion. The usual smell of gas may be destroyed By HE charge or deliberately disguised or mixed with smoke. Enemy gas tactics on the beaches and inland may be summarized as follows:

(1) A fierce bombardment of gas-containing shells lasting more than 2 minutes, by which the enemy will attempt to attain the maximum surprise;

(2) There may be long harrassing bombardments at a slow rate of fire designed to lower morale and gas discipline. But at any moment, the enemy may try a surprise shoot of fierce intensity;

(3) A small number of tear gas shells over long periods, also designed to lower morale and gas discipline; this also may be followed by a surprise shoot of great intensity when the enemy expects casualties among men who no longer trouble to adjust their masks quickly;

(4) The beaches may be contaminated. Belts of contamination are likely to be deep. Fake contamination may also be used.

(5) Chemical mines may be planted either with or separately from normal explosive mines;

(6) Gas may be mixed with smoke.

FLAME THROWERS

Flame throwers may be used by our forces and the enemy. They throw a stream of burning liquid and gas in small cones very like streams of water from high pressure fire hoses.

Their effective range is about 40 yards, and they are usually fired in bursts of from 2 to 3 seconds duration. These bursts will burn intensely for about 10 seconds.

Two general types may be encountered:

(a) Portable.

(1) Carried on the backs of men (2 to 3 men per flame thrower team). This equipment consists of tanks on the men's backs connected by a flexible hose to a small metal pole, known as the gun.

(2) In tanks and other armored vehicles mounted in place of a machine gun. The above types can be used in any direction.

FLAME THROWERS (Cont.)

   (b) Fixed.

        In pill boxes, strong points, defiles and at or near
        line. This type is usually fixed to fire in one
        direction by remote control.

   One charging of a flame thrower is only good for from 15 to 20
seconds continuous fire.

   Defense.

     (a) Stay out of cone of fire, or, if caught, hold your breath
        and roll out of the cone on either side.
     (b) Against portable type, kill the crew before they get in
        range. These men are easily recognized by the tanks on
        their backs.
     (c) Landing craft can successfully pass through, but should
        not head into, the **flame**, if all hands will remain well
        below the gunwales and the craft is moving at maximum
        speed. Men should hold their breath while the craft is
        passing through the flame.
     (d) Gas masks are no protection against flame throwers.

RADAR

   Types of enemy radar which might affect the Naval Assault Areas in future
amphibious operations are: Coastal Ship-watching Stations (C.W.) and Aircraft
Reporting Stations (A.R.S.), Nightfighter Control Stations (G.C.I.) and Benite
Dayfighter Control Stations (D.C.S.) are usually located several miles inland
and are not expected to affect naval operations.

   Types of Radar Installations are illustrated below:

S E C R E T

-30-

RADAR

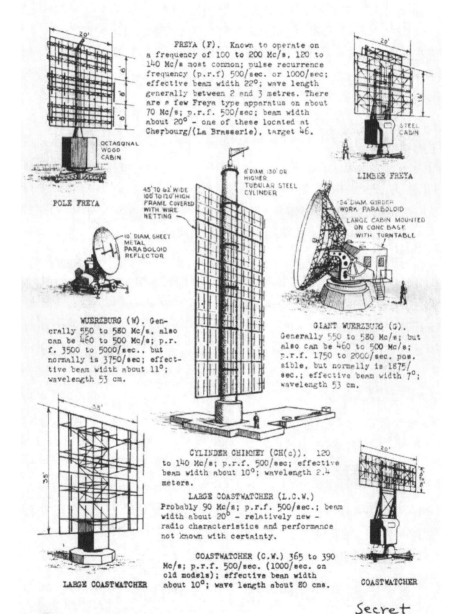

FREYA (F). Known to operate on a frequency of 100 to 200 Mc/s, 120 to 140 Mc/s most common; pulse recurrence frequency (p.r.f) 500/sec. or 1000/sec; effective beam width 22°; wave length generally between 2 and 3 metres. There are a few Freya type apparatus on about 70 Mc/s; p.r.f. 500/sec; beam width about 20° - one of these located at Cherbourg/(La Brasserie), target 46.

POLE FREYA

OCTAGONAL WOOD CABIN

LIMBER FREYA

STEEL CABIN

6' DIAM. 130' OR HIGHER TUBULAR STEEL CYLINDER

45' TO 62' WIDE 100' TO 120' HIGH FRAME COVERED WITH WIRE NETTING

10' DIAM. SHEET METAL PARABOLOID REFLECTOR

24' DIAM. GIRDER WORK PARABOLOID

LARGE CABIN MOUNTED ON CONC BASE WITH TURNTABLE

WUERZBURG (W). Generally 550 to 580 Mc/s, also can be 460 to 500 Mc/s; p.r.f. 3500 to 5000/sec., but normally is 3750/sec; effective beam width about 11°; wavelength 53 cm.

GIANT WUERZBURG (G). Generally 550 to 580 Mc/s; but also can be 460 to 500 Mc/s; p.r.f. 1750 to 2000/sec. possible, but normally is 1875/sec.; effective beam width 7°; wavelength 53 cm.

CYLINDER CHIMNEY (CH(c)). 120 to 140 Mc/s; p.r.f. 500/sec; effective beam width about 10°; wavelength 2.4 metres.

LARGE COASTWATCHER (L.C.W.) Probably 90 Mc/s; p.r.f. 500/sec.; beam width about 20° - relatively new - radio characteristics and performance not known with certainty.

COASTWATCHER (C.W.) 365 to 390 Mc/s; p.r.f. 500/sec. (1000/sec. on old models); effective beam width about 10°; wave length about 80 cms.

LARGE COASTWATCHER

COASTWATCHER

Secret

SURVIVAL INTELLIGENCE

A. Life Belt Notes:
1. Many of the men who lost their lives in a recent E-boat attack perished through improper use of their lifebelts. They were found floating head down, rump above the water, body bent over like a partially opened jack-knife. They had worn their life belts too low. They had inflated them with CO2 cartridges without loosening the belts to take care of the rapid expansion with inflation.
The dual pneumatic life belt, Type D, is the rubberized grayish khaki life belt with which most of our forces are equipped.
a. It should be worn loosely around the waist as high as is practicable.
b. Before inflation, the wearer should unfasten the snaps on the left side of the belt and raise the belt to chest level. This increases the circumference of the belt to take care of expansion with inflation.
c. Do not inflate before entering the water, as an inflated life belt can injure you if you have to jump from any height.
2. Kapok or coat-type life preservers should be held, not worn, if you are obliged to jump over the side, as either type can break your neck if worn when you jump from any height.

B. Abandoning Ship
1. Equipment
The best form of life insurance is proper equipment, all of which is simple and easily obtainable. The following are essential:
a. Leather, or leather palm, gloves - Fire is your greatest enemy in abandoning ship. Protect your hands while negotiating hot hand rails and going down lines.
b. Flash Light. Water proof it by enclosing it in rubber sheath (an ordinary contraceptive, or "rubber" will serve the purpose). Secure the flash-light to your person with aline.
c. Jack-knife or sheath knife - tie to you.
d. 3 or 4 feet of line - Have it available to lash yourself or a shipmate to a floating object, for use as a tourniquet, etc.
e. Your full canteen - Fastened to you.
f. Keep your clothes on. They will protect you from fire and exposure.

2. Jumping
a. Don't jump if you can get in the water by going down a net or line.
b. If you have to jump, keep your shoes on and jump feet first.
c. Carry your helmet and kapok or coat-type life jacket, because either can break your neck if you wear them while jumping.
d. Look out below. Don't jump on your shipmates or floating objects.
e. Jump from the windward side of the ship, as the ship will give way to the lee faster than a man can swim.
f. Jump from the bow or stern, whichever is lower in the water, but, if jumping from the stern, keep clear of the propellers.
g. Swim hard until you get clear of the ship, then breast stroke or back stroke to conserve your strength.
3. Swimming
a. If depth charges or bombs are exploding in the water, float or swim on your back, as this will protect you best against concussion effects.
b. Stay in groups. This will facilitate your being picked up.
c. Once clear of the ship, don't thrash around. Swim breast stroke or back stroke to save your strength.
4. Burning Oil
a. If you have to swim through burning oil, don't inflate your life belt or wear a coat type jacket. Swim under water under the flames as much as you can. When you must come up for air, flail around with your arms, as you come up, to clear a space.
b. Groups of swimmers should go through oil in line, if possible, with the stronger swimmers breaking the path.
5. Special Notes
a. Don't fasten the chin strap of your helmet. This may prevent your neck being broken during a bombardment.
b. When falling flat on the ground or in a fox-hole during bombing or bombardment, raise yourself slightly so you rest on elbows and knees. Keep your head and chin off the ground. Failure to do this may result in serious head or internal injuries.
c. Don't touch anything ashore which your duties don't require you to handle. Enemy held territory will probably have booby traps; souvenir hunting has cost many lives unnecessarily.

-31-   SECRET

File No. 3Grp8thPhib/A16-3(4)
Serial: 00070

TOP SECRET - BIGOT - ANVIL   1 August 1944

APPENDIX 2 to
ANNEX ABLE of
OPERATION PLAN
CTF 87 No. 1-44

REPORT PLAN

A. General

    1. The prompt dissemination of information to higher echelons is essential
during the operation. However, because of the limitations of communication
facilities and the necessity of having available frequencies specially
when "Urgent" messages need to be sent, it is imperative that: (1) each
message be written in as concise language as possible; (2) no unnecessary
message be sent; and (3) no repetition be made (unless called for. To
facilitate communications it is suggested that dispatch boats and visual
messages be used whenever possible.

    2. Intelligence officers from the staff of the Task Force Commander have
been assigned to Assault Group Commanders and AFA's to assist various
Group and Unit commanders in keeping informed of the situation, and in
passing on information to higher echelons. These officers shall be used
to the fullest advantage in the collection and dissemination of information.

    3. ESSENTIAL ELEMENTS OF INFORMATION DESIRED:

        a. The following classes of information will be reported to this
command as soon as practicable.
        (1) Location, disposition, speed and course of enemy units.
        (2) Loss or damage inflicted upon or by enemy units.
        (3) Beach information affecting landings and indicating conditions
markedly different than indicated by previous information. Immediate reconnaissance of the assault and near by beaches, with
emphasis on bars, gradients, rocks, etc., must be made as soon
as possible so that the most favorable location may be utilized
for the unloading of supplies.
        (4) Location and composition of previously unreported enemy mine-
fields, underwater obstacles, etc.
        (5) Location of control stations for minefields.
        (6) Location of enemy swept channels and areas.
        (7) Enemy plans and preparations for demolition and blocking of ports
and channels.
        (8) Location of enemy batteries, defenses, and radar stations not pre-
viously identified.
        (9) Any new type of enemy ship, weapon or device encountered.
        (10) Condition of ports, with emphasis on extent of demolition, con-
dition of channels, wrecks, etc., upon occupation of such ports.
        (11) Estimated capacity of ports upon occupation.
        (12) Enemy plans or intentions.
        (13) Enemy use of, or intention to use, toxic gases, and beach contami-
nation agents.
        (14) Enemy order of battle; methods, and effectiveness of enemy
defenses.
        (15) Reaction of local population to the invasion.
        (16) Enemy espionage and sabotage activities and intentions in respect
thereto.
        (17) Damage inflicted by Allied bombing, naval gunfire, rocket fire,
etc.

APPENDIX 2 to
ANNEX ABLE
REPORT PLAN

File:
3Grp8thPhib/A16-3(4)
Serial: 00070

1 August 1944

TOP SECRET - BIGOT - ANVIL

APPENDIX 2 to
ANNEX ABLE of
OPERATION PLAN
CTF 87 No. 1-44

REPORT PLAN

B. Current Reports During the Operation.

a. REPORTS BY ALL SHIPS AND STATIONS TO THE TASK FORCE COMMANDER CTF 87 AND THE APPROPRIATE GROUP COMMANDER.

  (1). Immediately upon contact with, sighting of, or attack by the enemy, (within limitations of radio silence) giving:
    (a). Time of contact, sighting or attack.
    (b). Size of the enemy force.
    (c). Description of enemy force.
    (d). If U-boat, whether or not surfaced.
    (e). Location of reporting agency (if necessary).
    (f). True bearing of enemy.
    (g). If airborne, altitude (in feet) of enemy.
    (h). Distance (in yards) of enemy.
    (i). Speed (in knots) of enemy.
    (j). Course (degrees true) of enemy.
    (k). Pertinent additional information.

  (2). Immediately upon being damaged (with due regards to limitations of radio silence), giving:
    (a). Time damage occurred.
    (b). How damage was inflicted.
    (c). Estimate of damage.
    (d). What craft are standing by.
    (e). What assistance is needed.
    (f). Pertinent additional information.

  (3). Immediately when landing is made on other than the assigned beach, giving:
    (a). Exact location of beach where landing is made.
    (B). Obstacles encountered (natural and man-made).
    (c). Enemy resistance.

  (4) Immediately when landing has been repulsed, giving:
    (a). Time of repulse.
    (b). Reason for repulse.
    (c). Type of resistance encountered.
    (d). Losses of craft, men vehicles, and supplies (in tons).
    (e). Pertinent additional information.

  (5) Immediately when beach is closed, giving:
    (a). Actual time of closing.
    (b). Types of craft beach is closed to.
    (c). Reason for closing.
    (d). Pertinent additional information.

File No.   3Grp8thPhib/A16-3(4)
Serial: 00070

TOP SECRET - BIGOT - ANVIL

APPENDIX 2 to   1 August 1944
ANNEX ABLE of
OPERATION PLAN
CTF 87 No. 1-44

REPORT PLAN

    (6). Immediately upon taking prisoners or captured documents aboard,
unless this fact has been previously reported, giving:
    (a) Description of what has been taken aboard.
    (b) Number taken aboard.
    (c) Pertinent additional information.

    (7) Immediately when the enemy is known to be using gas, giving:
    (a) Where it is being used.
    (b) Methods used.
    (c) Type gas used.
    (d) Apparent effect on Allied Forces in the area.

    (8) Immediately when radio silence is broken or thereafter when
enemy mining activity is suspected in the area, giving the
following information in the following form:
    (a) ABLE - Time of occurrence.
    (b) BAKER - Description of occurrence.
        ONE - Floating mine observed.
        TWO - Parachute mine observed.
       THREE - Ship striking moored mine.
       FOUR - Ship mined by ground mine.
       FIVE - Sweeper cutting moored mine.
       SIX - Sweeper detonating ground mine.
     SEVEN - Detection of mine by sound gear.
    (c) CHARLIE - Latitude and longitude of occurrence.
    (d) DOG - Whether position is being buoyed.
    (e) EASY - Degree of reliability.
        ONE - Certain
        TWO - Probable
      THREE- Possible
      FOUR - Doubtful

    (9) Medical reports shall be submitted in accordance with
Appendix I to Annex NAN, Medical Reports.

b. REPORTS BY THE ASSAULT GROUP COMMANDERS TO THE ASSAULT FORCE COMMAND-
ER.
    (1) On D-day at H plus 3 hours and every 4 hours thereafter, (more
regularly if advisable) and after D-day at 1200 and 1800 only, an
unloading progress report should be made, giving:
    (a) Troops disembarked since last report.
    (b) Vehicles unloaded.
    (c) Stores (in tons) unloaded.
    (d) Brief summary of conditions on the beach.
    (2) At 1100 and 1700 Daily reports should be made on number and
type craft in outbound Convoy Assembly Area.

APPENDIX 2 to
ANNEX ABLE
REPORT PLAN

File No. 3Grp8thPhib/A16-3(4)
Serial: 00070

TOP SECRET - BIGOT - ANVIL

APPENDIX 2 to
ANNEX ABLE   1 August 1944
OPERATION PLAN
CTF 87 No. 1-44

REPORT PLAN

    c. REPORTS BY ALL SHIPS UNDER THE COMMAND OF THE ASSAULT GROUP COMMAND-
        ERS TO THE APPROPRIATE ASSAULT GROUP COMMANDER.

        (1) On D-day at H plus 2½ hours and every 4 hours thereafter, (more
regularly if advisable) and after D-day at 1100 and 1700 an unloading
progress report should be made, giving:
        (a) Troops disembarked.
        (b) Vehicles unloaded.
        (c) Stores (in tons) unloaded.

        (2) Whenever completely unloaded they should report this fact.

        (3) Immediately upon the return from the beach of small craft a
brief summary of conditions on the beach should be submitted
including:
        (a) Enemy resistance.
        (b) Allied situation.
        (c) Underwater obstacles.
        (d) Landing conditions.

        (4) A daily report by 0900 giving details of enemy air attack
during the night.

    d. REPORTS BY THE NAVAL BEACH PARTY TO THE ASSAULT FORCE COMMANDER AND
        THE APPROPRIATE ASSAULT GROUP COMMANDER.
        (1) 20 minutes after landing and every 4 hours thereafter progress
reports giving any intelligence obtained, including:
        (a) Friendly and enemy situation.
        (b) Underwater obstacles, mines, etc.
        (c) Landing condition.

        (2) Whenever it is deemed advisable, report on broached boats,
giving:
        (a) Type craft.
        (b) Hull numbers.
        (c) Whether or not salvageable.
        (d) Cause of damage.

        (3) At 1700 daily, an unloading progress report, giving:
        (a) Troops disembarked in last 24 hours.
        (b) Vehicles unloaded in last 24 hours.
        (c) Stores (in tons) unloaded in last 24 hours.

APPENDIX 2 to
ANNEX ABLE
REPORT PLAN

File No.   3Grp8thPhib/A16-3(4)
Serial: 00070

TOP SECRET - BIGOT - ANVIL   1 August 1944

APPENDIX 2 to
ANNEX ABLE
OPERATION PLAN
CTF 87 No. 1-44

REPORT PLAN

    e.   REPORTS BY THE PRIMARY CONTROL VESSELS TO THE ASSAULT FORCE COMMANDER
AND THE APPROPRIATE ASSAULT GROUP COMMANDERS.
        (1)   Immediately after the first and last waves hit the beach,
giving:
            (a) Wave number.
            (b) Time of hitting the beach.
            (c) Place of hitting the beach.
            (d) Craft missing from wave and extra craft in wave, if any.

        (2)   At H plus 45 minutes and every hour thereafter, **variances** from
scheduled wave landings, in, (a) time of landing, (b) place of
landing, (c) type and number of craft landing, will be reported.
(If the variance is of sufficient importance, it should be
reported immediately.) This report should also include miscellaneous craft making unscheduled landings.

        (3)   At H plus 30 minutes and as often thereafter as needed, gener-
al intelligence reports should be submitted, giving:
            (a) Surf conditions.
            (b) Amount and type of obstacles.
            (c) Amount and type of opposition encountered.
            (d) Observed effect of Naval gunfire and rocket support.
            (e) Pertinent additional information, including: (a) time
of landing of waves observed, (b) number of boats lost, and
type of damage to Allied men and material.

        (4)   Immediately after the assault is over a list should be sub-
mitted giving:
            (a) Time of landing of all waves.
            (b) Number and type of craft lost.
            (c) An estimate of the loss of men, vehicles, and supplies
(in tons).

    f.   REPORTS BY ALL CONTROL AND REFERENCE VESSELS TO THE TASK FORCE
COMMANDER

        (1)   Immediately after the operation is over or when called for,
a record, giving:
            (a) Composition of all passing waves.
            (b) Time of passing of each wave.
            (c) where possible, time of landing of each wave.

    g.   REPORTS BY ALL BOAT WAVE COMMANDERS TO THE APPROPRIATE PRIMARY
CONTROL VESSEL.

APPENDIX 2 to
ANNEX ABLE
REPORT PLAN

File No.   3Grp8thPhib/A16-3(4)
Serial: 00070

TOP SECRET - BIGOT - ANVIL   1 August 1944

APPENDIX 2 to
ANNEX ABLE
OPERATION PLAN
CTF 87 No. 1-44

REPORT PLAN

        (1) As soon as the wave is clear of the beach, giving:
           (a) Surf conditions.
           (b) Amount and type of obstacles.
           (c) Amount and type of opposition encountered.
           (d) Observed effect of Naval gunfire and rocket support.
           (e) Pertinent additional information, including: (a) time of
landing of wave, (b) number of boats lost, and (c) amount and
type of damage to Allied men and material.

h.   REPORTS BY THE COMMANDER BOMBARDMENT GROUP TO THE ASSAULT FORCE
COMMANDER.

        (1) When individual ammunition expended reaches 70% of individual
allowance.

        (2) At 1200 daily starting D plus 1, a report of percentage of
ammunition remaining on board.

        (3) At 1715 daily starting D-day, a report on aircraft spotting
requirements for the following day should be made.

        (4) At 1800 daily a brief of gunfire support with an assessment
of the effect of fire if known.

        (5) A daily report of enemy air activity during the night.

i.   REPORT BY SENIOR DEMOLITION OFFICER ON EACH BEACH TO ASSAULT FORCE
AND TO ASSAULT GROUP COMMANDER
        (1) As soon as practicable after H-hour.
           (a) The number of gaps cut through the obstacles and the
approximate width of each gap.
           (b) Total percentage of beach remaining to be cleared of
obstacles.

j.   REPORT BY ALL MINESWEEPERS TO TASK FORCE COMMANDER

        (1) In accordance with NCWTF Operation Order, Appendix II to
Annex JIG (Minesweeping Plan).

k.   REPORT BY OFFICER-IN-CHARGE SALVAGE AND FIRE FIGHTING TO TASK FORCE
COMMANDER.
        (1) Daily, until D / 10, thereafter weekly, submit a chronological
list of salvage work since last report.

Page 6 of 7   APPENDIX 2 to
                                               ANNEX ABLE
                                               REPORT PLAN

File No.   3Grp8thPhib/A16-3(4)
Serial: 00070

TOP SECRET - BIGOT - ANVIL

APPENDIX 2 to   1 August 1944
ANNEX ABLE
OPERATION PLAN
CTF 87 No. 1-44

REPORT PLAN

    1. REPORT BY THE LANDING CRAFT SALVAGE OFFICER TO THE TASK FORCE
    COMMANDER
      (1) Maintain a record and be prepared to submit same on call, giving:
        (a) Number and type of craft repaired and returned to service.
        (b) Number and type of craft turned over to towing vessels.
        (c) Number and type of craft damaged beyond repair.

    m. REPORTS BY ALL INCOMING CONVOY COMMODORES TO TASK FORCE COMMANDER

      (1) Immediately upon arrival in Transport area, giving:

        (a) Variances from schedule in name, type and/or number of
        ships.
        (b) Pertinent additional information.

      (2) As soon as practicable, when it is known that convoy arrival
      is behind schedule, dispatch a fast boat to inform CTF 87 estimat-
      ed time of arrival.

N:

S-E-C-R-E-T

PROCEDURE OF THE N-2 SECTION

On 25 June 1944, Group 2, 11th Amphibious Force, under command of Rear Admiral Don P. MOON, USN. completed its duties in the assault on the CHERBOURG PENINSULA in Operation NEPTUNE, and the Flagship, USS BAYFIELD returned to PLYMOUTH, DEVON, ENGLAND, with the Staff aboard. Admiral MOON immediately reported to COMNAVEU in LONDON where he received orders to report with his staff to COMNAVNAW for duty and to prepared for Operation DRAGOON, proposed Allied Assault on the Southern Coast of France.

On 29 June 1944 Admiral MOON and an Advance Section of the Staff departed PLYMOUTH by air for the MEDITERRANEAN THEATER, arriving the next afternoon in ALGIERS, where COMNAVNAW, Vice Admiral HEWITT, USN. gave Admiral MOON orders to serve as Commander Group 3, 8th Amphibious Force, and to prepare to participate in Operation DRAGOON as Commander of Task Force 87. The next day the Admiral and the Advance Section of the Staff arrived in NAPLES, ITALY, and immediately moved into the BLACKHOUSE which was to serve as headquarters for the planners of all forces participating in the new operation.

The remainder of the Staff left PLYMOUTH aboard the BAYFIELD 5 July 1944, arriving in NAPLES 15 July 1944.

The N-2 Section of the Staff consisted of the Staff Intelligence Officer, Lt. Comdr. Robert M. Thayer, USNR. and 14 Assistant Intelligence Officers including an Assistant Intelligence Officer for Air and two Photo Interpreters. Each officer was assigned a specific subject for specialized study in accordance with his experience in the previous operation. In addition, certain officers were assigned the duty of maintaining liaison with the various types of ships and craft assigned to the Task Force.

The names of the Assistant Intelligence Officers together with their assignments are listed below:

Name	Duties	Craft/Ship Liaison
Lt.Comdr. Ellery Sedgwick, USNR.	Executive Officer / Enemy Batteries	Bombardment Group
Lt. Rupert M. Allan, USNR.	Enemy Air	Carriers
Lt. Thomas J. Hughes, USNR.	Enemy Order of Battle	Beach Battalion
Lt. Sam R. Sanders, USNR.	Enemy Surface Forces	LSTs.
Lt. Harry C. Midgley, USNR.	Underwater Obstacles	Beach Battalion and Demolition Units.
Lt. Charles L. Burwell, USNR.	Beach Studies	
Lt. G. Budd Palmer, USNR.	Beach Studies	LCI(L)s
Lt. Alvan D. Turquette, USNR.	Photo Interpreter	
Lt. M. M. Parrish, Jr., USNR.	Enemy Marine Mines	Control Vessels
Lt. Harold I. McGowan, USNR.	Enemy Strongpoints	Gunfire Support Craft
Lt. Donald G. McNeil, USNR.	Coastal Terrain and Ass't Enemy Air	LCTs
Lt.(jg) Richard B. Tucker, USNR.	Enemy Submarines and Enemy Weapons	Screening Ships
Lt.(jg) Mark Dalton, USNR.	Administration Officer and War Diary.	
Lt.(jg) Douglas E. Brogden, USNR.	Ass't Photo Interpreter	

- 1 -

File No: 3G8thPhib/A16-3(4)
Serial: 00070

<u>TOP SECRET - BIGOT - ANVIL</u>   1 August 1944

<u>ANNEX ABLE</u> of
<u>OPERATION PLAN</u>
CTF 87 No. 1-44

<u>INTELLIGENCE PLAN</u>   <u>TABLE OF CONTENTS</u>

PAGE 1 of 1 PAGE   - 1 -   <u>ANNEX ABLE</u>
                                             <u>INTELLIGENCE PLAN - TABLE OF CONTENTS</u>

File No.
3Gr8thPhib/A16-3(4)

Serial: 00070   1 August 1944.

TOP SECRET - BIGOT - ANVIL

ANNEX "ABLE" of
OPERATION PLAN
CTF 87 No. 1-44

INTELLIGENCE PLAN

1. This Annex is informative in character, and none of the material herein is to be
   considered as a directive.

2. Information regarding location and characteristics of Enemy Air and Surface Forces,
   Weapons, and Tactics has been prepared in a separate pamphlet which has been previously distributed to all units of this Task Force. This information is not
   repeated in this Annex. Information on Ports will be found in Information Annex
   to Naval Commander Western Task Force Operation Plan 4-44.

3. Naval Commander Western Task Force has prepared beach sketches with descriptive
   texts of the Assault Beaches, maps with overprints of strong points and coastal
   batteries, and special photographs of appropriate areas; these will be distributed
   to all units. The information in this Annex should be read in conjunction with
   the material prepared by NCWTF, Operation Order 4-44;

4. Last minute changes in the disposition of enemy forces and any other additional
   information of importance will be disseminated by despatch.

5. If any information promulgated by NCWTF or higher authority conflicts with that
   contained in this Annex, the former should be accepted.

Page 1 of 16

ANNEX "ABLE" of OPERATION PLAN
CTF 87. No. 1-44
INTELLIGENCE PLAN

File No.
  3Gr8thPhib/A16-3(4)

Serial: 00070   1 August 1944.

TOP SECRET - DICOT - ANVIL

ANNEX "ABLE" of
OPERATION PLAN
CTF 87 No. 1-44

INTELLIGENCE PLAN

A. Operation ANVIL is a three divisional attack against the South coast of FRANCE in
    order to secure a bridgehead and capture the ports of TOULON and MARSEILLES.

B. Task Force 87 will land the 36th Division on three beaches, RED, GREEN, and BLUE
    (numbered 264-A, 264-B, and 265-A) situated along a stretch of the Southeastern
    Coast of FRANCE between the GULF OF FREJUS and a point 1½ miles east of RADE
    D'AGAY. YELLOW Beach (number 265) will possibly be developed after H-hour if
    circumstances so require.

I. ASSAULT AREA TERRAIN

    A. NARROW COASTAL LOWLANDS.

        The assault area is located on narrow coastal lowlands which are backed by the
        dry and desolate Southern Alps. Terrain altitudes of 300 feet and under are
        found only for a few miles inland. At FREJUS this low country extends about
        5 miles inland. At CAVALAIRE it extends less than a mile, and there are
        promontaries rising over 1,000 feet within a mile of the coast line.

    B. THE SOUTHERN ALPS.

        The Southern Alps to the North behind the landing areas are very sparsely
        populated. There is no industry in that region, and very little agriculture.
        The terrain consists of rugged limestone heights varying in altitude from 600
        to 6000 feet. Fifty miles to the Northeast the MARITIME Alps rise over
        10,000 feet above sea level. The largest town to the North inland is GAP
        which had a pre-war population of only 13,000.

    C. VALLEY OF THE ARGENS.

        West of FREJUS are the two major French ports of TOULON and MARSEILLES.
        TOULON is about 50 miles West of FREJUS and MARSEILLES about 30 miles West
        of TOULON. A valley runs from FREJUS to TOULON and connects these two
        coastal towns. The valley describes a moderate arc inland, and is about 18
        miles from the coast at its farthest point. Through this valley runs the
        major railroad which connects NICE and CANNES in the East and TOULON and
        MARSEILLES in the West. Through it also runs the major roadway. There is
        also a coastal road, which connects FREJUS and TOULON, and a single track
        narrow gauge railway, which runs along the coast between the two places.

II. ASSAULT BEACH STUDY.

    A. GREEN BEACH (No. 264-B)

        This beach extends for 840 yards along the Western side of CAP DRAMMONT, 4
        miles East of ST. RAPHAEL and the GULF OF FREJUS, and immediately West of
        RADE D'AGAY on the Southeastern coast of FRANCE. The midpoint of this beach
        (43° 24' 57" N; 06° 50' 42" E) is 73 air miles from MARSEILLES, 50 air miles
        from TOULON, and about 500 air miles from NAPLES.

ANNEX "ABLE" of OPERATION PLAN
CTF 87, No. 1-44
INTELLIGENCE PLAN

File No.
.3gr8thPhib/A16-3(4)

Serial: 00070

1 August 1944,

TOP SECRET - PIGOT - ANVIL

ANNEX "ABLE" of
OPERATION PLAN
CTF 87 No. 1-44

INTELLIGENCE PLAN

1. Location.
   Coordinates

   207512 to 214510

2. Length

   840 yards,

3. Width (from back of beach to waterline)

   25 yards West end
   22 yards center
   16 yards Eastern end.

4. Slope (Gradient).

   The gradient of the beach from the 1 fathom line to the waterline
   is 1:20.

5. Nature of the beach.

   a. Consistency – This beach is composed of sand and gravel and is
      flanked by a rocky shoreline. Traction should be sufficient
      for tracked vehicles, but wheeled vehicles probably could not
      negotiate the beach without using matting.

6. Cover.

   There is cover to be found on the Western end of the beach at the
   base of an embankment 8-10 feet high, at the base of the vertical
   face of quarry working 35-40 feet high at the center of the beach,
   and at the base of the high cliff forming the Eastern flank of the
   beach.

7. Exits.

   At the extreme Eastern end of the beach there is a track which
   leads across broken ground and connects with a minor road at 214511.
   This minor road connects with a main coastal road. Tracked vehicles
   should not have much difficulty negotiating this exit, but preparation would be necessary for wheeled vehicles.

8. Landmarks.

   There are good distinguishing landmarks on GREEN BEACH. From seaward on the right flank of the beach, the red cliff of CAP DRAMMONT,
   rising 482 feet, is clearly visible. The ILE D'OR, a small, low,
   rocky island slightly West of CAP DRAMMONT, has a conspicuous
   square white tower upon it. There are low, red cliffs directly
   behind the center of the beach, and immediately on each flank there
   are rocky formations. The heavily forested mountains of ESTEREL
   rise to heights of 500 feet within 1000 yards North of the beach.

Page 3 of 16

File No.
3Gr8thPhib/A16-3(4)

Serial: 00070   1 August 1944.

TOP SECRET - BIGOT Q ANVIL

ANNEX "ABLE" of
OPERATION PLAN
CTF 87 No. 1-44

INTELLIGENCE PLAN

There is a small boat harbor between the beach and the cliff of CAP
DRAMMONT. This harbor is probably too shallow for LCVP's.

The main coastal road and railway lie 100 to 200 yards inland of the
beach. An embankment 8-10 feet high supports this coastal road
immediately behind the Western end of the beach, but at the center of
the beach and to the East this embankment merges into the rough vertical face of quarry workings. There is a loading conveyor or pipe-
line that rises to the top of the cliff immediately behind the center
of the beach.

9. Approach.

The approach is clear from the Southwest, but from the South it is
blocked above and below the surface by rocks extending 330 yards
from the ILE D'OR. There is a rock on the seabed close inshore at
either end of the beach.

The 50 fathom line lies 4300 yards off the beach.
    " 20 "   "   "   600   "   "   "   "
    " 10 "   "   "   300   "   "   "   "
    "   5 "   "   "   150   "   "   "   "
    "   3 "   "   "   75   "   "   "   "

10.   Anchorage.

    a. Offshore – There is no anchorage in less than 100 fathoms more
        than 2 miles off the beach.

    b. Inshore – There is poor anchorage over mud and weed in 10
        fathoms 300 yards off the beach.

11.   Landing.

    All types of amphibious craft will beach without difficulty. Men
    and vehicles will move short distances through 1 to 2 feet of water
    from the beached craft to dry land.

B. BLUE BEACH (No. 265-A)

    This beach (43° 26.2' N; 06° 53.6' E) at GALANQUE D'ANTHEOR on the
    Southeastern coast of France extends for 80 yards at the head of a
    small cove. It is 6 miles East of ST. RAPHAEL, and 1½ miles East of
    AGAY. It is 73 air miles from MARSEILLES, 48 air miles from TOULON and
    about 500 air miles from NAPLES.

Page 4 of 16   ANNEX ABLE of OPERATION PLAN
                                            CTF 87, No. 1-44
                                            INTELLIGENCE PLAN

File No.
3Gr8thPhib/A16-3(4)

Serial: 00070

1 August 1944.

TOP SECRET - BIGOT - ANVIL

ANNEX "ABLE" of
OPERATION PLAN
CTF 87 No. 1-44

INTELLIGENCE PLAN

1. Location.
   Coordinate   254531

2. Length.   80 yards.

3. Width (from back of beach to waterline) 15 yards Northeast end
                                            30 yards Center
                                            15 yards Southwest end.

4. Slope (Gradient).

   The slope of the beach above the waterline is 1:15, while from
   the waterline to the 2 fathom line it is 1:40.

5. Nature of Beaches.

   a. Consistency – This is a fine sand beach which lies at the
      head of a cove bordered by steep, rocky sides. The sand is
      soft and loose, and even tracked vehicles might experience
      difficulty. It is definitely impracticable for wheeled
      vehicles unless mats are laid.

   b. Seaweed – With Easterly or Southerly winds, banks of seaweed
      up to 4 feet in depth are deposited on this narrow beach.

6. Cover.

   There is cover for infantry at the base of the road embankment
   and on the wooded slopes which rise inland from the beach.
   Cover for vehicles is scarce, and it is probably only available
   for small numbers in the gardens of houses along the coast road.

7. Exits.

   Infantry can move straight off the beach on to a coast road
   (20-25 feet wide), but a ramp will have to be built to enable
   vehicles to gain the road.

8. Landmarks.

   Just inland of the coast road there is a masonry railway bridge,
   60 feet high, with 9 large arches. This bridge spans the
   cliffs on either side of the deep, narrow valley backing the
   beach. The sides of this valley are deeply scarred by bomb
   craters resulting from the bombing of this vital railway bridge.
   There are several houses on the banks of the valley.

ANNEX "ABLE" of OPERATION PLAN
                                            CTF 87, No. 1-44
                                            INTELLIGENCE PLAN

File No.
    3Gr8thihib/A16-3(4)

Serial: 00070   1 August 1944.

TOP SECRET - BIGOT - ANVIL

ANNEX "ABLE" of
OPERATION PLAN
CTF 87 No. 1-44.

INTELLIGENCE PLAN

        9. Approach.

            The beach is located about 250 yards in from the entrance to the
            cove. The approach to the voce is clear to the Southeast. The
            entrance to the cove is 300 yards wide between rocky points.
            Just off either flank of the beach there is submerged rock ex-
            tending all the way to the cove entrance, so that the clear
            passage for craft is only about 80 yards wide.

            The 50 fathom line lies 2500 yards off the beach.

"	25	"	"	"	1200	"	"	"	"
"	10	"	"	"	600	"	"	"	"
"	5	"	"	"	250	"	"	"	"

     10. Anchorage.

            Exposed anchorage can be found in 5 fathoms over sand, 350 yards
            Southeast of the beach.

     11. Landing.

            This beach and its approaches are too narrow to enable any
            amphibious craft larger than LCMs to maneuver.

    C. RED BEACH (No. 264-A)

        This beach extends for 850 yards along the Northern half of the low, flat
        shore between the town of ST. RAPHAEL and the rocky head land of POINTE
        ST. AYGULF, in the GULF OF FREJUS on the Southeastern coast of FRANCE.
        The midpoint of this beach (43° 25' 18" N; 06° 45' 12" E) is 68 air miles
        from MARSEILLES, 45 air miles from TOULON, and about 500 air miles from
        NAPLES.

      1. Location.
          Coordinates   573342 to 568337

      2. Length.   850 yards.

      3. Width (from back of beach to waterline).   50 yards at North end.
                                         30 yards at South end.

      4. Slope (Gradient).

          From 2 fathom line to waterline   1:30
          From waterline to seawall   1:25

ANNEX "ABLE" of OPERATION PLAN
CTF 87, No. 1-44
INTELLIGENCE PLAN

File No.
    3Gr8thPhib/A16-3(4)

Serial: 00070   1 August 1944.

.TOP SECRET - BIGOT & ANVIL

ANNEX "ABLE" of
OPERATION PLAN
CTF 87. No. 1-44

INTELLIGENCE PLAN

    5. Nature of Beach.

        a. Consistency — This beach is composed of fine sand which will
            probably accomodate tracked vehicles but will require mats for
            wheeled vehicles.

        b. Jetties – There are 4 small jetties (or piers) near the South end
            of the beach, the largest of these comprising the Southern limit
            of the beach. This jetty extends for 465 feet from the seawall,
            is 36 feet wide, and rises 3 to 4 feet above water level. There
            are depths of about 12 feet at its outer end. It is doubtful if
            the 3 subsidiary jetties would prove useful for unloading craft.

        c. Seawall – A new anti-tank concrete wall (reportedly non-reinforced)
            extends the entire length of the assault beach and beyond into the
            Port of ST. RAPHAEL. This wall behind RED Beach is 5 feet high and
            3 feet thick and has an almost vertical face; there appear to be
            buttresses or braces 20 to 30 feet apart on the landward side of
            the left flank of the beach. Beyond RED Beach and extending
            almost to the small port of ST. RAPHAEL, the wall is in the shape
            of a row of concrete pillars about 3 feet apart.

    6. Cover.

        There is cover immediately in front of the seawall although this is
        open to enfilading fire.

    7. Exits.

        There are no prepared exits for vehicles from the assault beach, but
        there are gaps in the wall behind the first and third of the four
        jetties. The gaps are being blocked. If the wall is breached else-
        where, there is access on to the FREJUS-RAPHAEL road, which runs
        parallel to the Northern part of the beach, or on to an air field
        situated behind the South end of the beach. From this air field there
        is an outlet to the same road running Northwestward to FREJUS, 1 mile
        inland.

    8. Landmarks.

        From seaward the red cliffs of CAP DRAMMONT to the east rise 482 feet
        high and there is a conspicuous square white tower on the ILE D'OR.
        To the South, there is the wooded, rocky headland of CAP ST. AYGULF.
        To the West of CAP DRAMMONT, and visible as you approach, are the white
        hotels, churches, and the houses of the town of ST. RAPHAEL, about 1500
        yards Northeast of the beach. The Northern . 500 yards of the beach
        is backed by flat open country with scattered buildings and some marsh-
        land. The Southern 350 yards of the beach, formerly a seaplane base,
        is immediately backed by marshy land; this marshy land is to seaward
        of the airfield. Immediately to the North of the airfield and marking
        the North end of the assault beach is a large hotel close to the shore.
        About 1000 yards Southwest of the assault beach is the mouth of the
        ARGENS River with a large group of trees, the VILLA DES SABLES, on the
        Northeast bank.

A NNEX "ABLE" of OPERATION PLAN
CTF 87 No. 1-44
INTELLIGENCE PLAN

File No.
3Gr8thPhib/A16-3(4)

Serial: 00070   1 August 1944.

TOP SECRET - BIGOT - ANVIL

ANNEX "ABLE" of
OPERATION PLAN
CTF 87 No. 1-44

INTELLIGENCE PLAN

   9. Approach.

        The approach is clear from the South, but in approaching from the East,
        care must be taken to avoid the small, low, rocky island of LE LION SUR
        MER, 1000 yards offshore and about 1½ miles South-Southeast of ST.
        RAPHAEL.

        The 100 fathom line lies 9300 yards off the beach.
         "   50   "   "   "   " 3600   "   "   "   "
         "   20   "   "   "   " 1600   "   "   "   "
         "   10   "   "   "   "   850   "   "   "   "
         "   5   "   "   "   "   100   "   "   "   "
         "   5   "   "   "   "   300   "   "   "   "
        The 15 foot line lies 50 yards off the North end of the beach and 150
        yards off the South end of the beach.

   10. Sand-bars - Several months ago, a cusp-shaped sand-bar extended North
        for 350 yards from the South end of the beach. This bar was 200 feet
        offshore, with 1 to 2 feet of water over it and 2 to 4 feet of water
        inside it. The sand-bar has recently disappeared, but, subject to
        conditions of the sea, it may reappear at any time.

   11. Obstacles (man-made). Underwater obstacles in position off the entire
        length of RED Beach on 17 July 1944 consist of a single row of solid
        concrete pyramids placed 80 to 420 feet offshore in 6 to 8 feet of
        water, 10 to 18 feet apart. These pyramids are about 5 feet high, and
        3 feet wide at the base.

   12. Anchorage.

        There is a good anchorage over mud and weed in 5 to 7 fathoms, 500
        yards off the beach.

   13. Landing.

        All types of landing craft and LSTs can beach without difficulty.
        Men and vehicles will move short distances through 1 to 2 feet of
        water from beached craft to dry land.

 · D. YELLOW BEACH (No. 265)

        This beach is located in the RADE D'AGAY 5 miles East of ST. RAPHAEL on
        the Southeast coast of FRANCE. The RADE D'AGAY is a semi-circular bay,
        1300 yards deep, with 900 yards between the rocky flanks of the entrance.

        1. Location.

            Coordinates

            . East end   .   234526
               West end   225525
               Center   43° 26' 00" N; 06° 51' 46" E.

ANNEX "ABLE" of OPERATION PLAN
                                         CTF 87 No. 1-44
                                         INTELLIGENCE PLAN

File No.
3Gr8thPhib/A16-3(4)

Serial: 00070   1 August 1944.

TOP SECRET - BIGOT - ANVIL

ANNEX "ABLE" of
OPERATION PLAN
CTF 87 No. 1-44

INTELLIGENCE PLAN

2. Length   1300 yards

3. Width (from back of beach to waterline). East end 40 yards.
                                              Center 20 yards
                                              West end 40 yards.

4. Slope (Gradient).

    West sector   1:50
    Center   1:30
    East sector   1:40

5. Nature of Beach.

    a. Consistency – It is a semicircular beach of coarse sand and is
        bounded on the East by the CHATEAU D'AGAY and on the West by a
        small boat harbor. Tracked vehicles will probably be able to
        negotiate the sand, but without preparation, the beach is too
        soft for wheeled vehicles.

    b. Seawall – Beginning at the West end of the beach there is a ver-
        tical masonary seawall about 15 feet high; this seawall later
        becomes the abutment of a reinforced-concrete bridge across the
        mouth of the AGAY River. Across the bridge to the Northeast
        there runs an embankment which supports the coast road and grad-
        ually loses height until in the center of the beach there is no
        difference in level between the beach and the road. The Eastern
        half of the beach is backed only by a low bank overgrown with
        vegetation. The bank leads up to the main coast road.

6. Cover.

    There is good cover for infantry and vehicles among the houses,
    gardens, and trees of the village of AGAY. This village stretches
    along most of the beach Northwest of CHATEAU D'AGAY, and the cover
    is accessible to vehicles by means of roads leading up to houses on
    the foothills behind the beach.

7. Exits.

    For 200 yards from the Western end of the beach there is a 15 foot
    seawall. On the rest of the beach there are good exits for infantry
    at any point; but some preparation will be necessary for the movement
    of vehicles up over the embankment to the coast road.

8. Landmarks.

    From seaward, the red cliffs of CAP DRAMMONT, rising 482 feet above
    sea level, are conspicuous on the left flank of the 900 yard entrance t
    to the bay at the head of which lies the beach. POINTE DE LA BEAU-
    METTE, low in elevation and about 1 mile Northeastward, forms the

Page 9 of 16   ANNEX "ABLE" of OPERATION PLAN
                                      CTF 87 No. 1-44
                                      INTELLIGENCE PLAN

File No.
3Gr8thPhib/A16-3(4)

Serial: 00070   1 August 1944.

TOP SECRET - BIGOT - ANVIL

ANNEX "ABLE" of
OPERATION PLAN
CTF 87 No. 1-44

INTELLIGENCE PLAN

          right flank of the entrance to the bay. LE RASTEL D'AGAY, a range of
reddish hills from 850 to 1000 feet high, overlooks the beach from the
Northward.

    9. Approach.

        The approach from the South is clear. The entrance to the bay is 900
yards wide and has a channel of at least 5 fathoms deep and 600 yards
wide. 1300 yards from the entrance at the head of the bay, the 5
fathom line lies 300 yards offshore. The shores of the bay are
bordered by a rocky ledge, which has depths of less than 3 fathoms
over it and in places extends 250 yards offshore.

    10. Anchorage.

        Large vessels can anchor in depths of from 8 to 9 fathoms Southwest-
ward of the CHATEAU D'AGAY. Small vessels can anchor in depths of
from 4 to 5 fathoms about 300 yards off the beach at the head of the
bay. These anchorages over a bottom of mud covered with weed afford
good holding ground.

    11. Landing.

        All types of landing craft and LSTs can beach without difficulty.

III   WEATHER SEA AND SURF

    A. Weather

        Weather in this area is very uncertain the year around, and is subject
to violent change. It is highly localized and great difference in
weather conditions may be expected on beaches at short distances apart.
During the months of July, August, and September onshore winds are rare
and assault forces should normally be protected by the land masses. As
a rule, due to this condition, surf is not excessively high and should
not be a material hazard.

    B. Wind

        Prevailing winds are, in general, Westerly. There is a well defined
pattern of offshore and onshore breezes. Land breeze usually starts at
sunset and increases to a maximum at daybreak. The sea breeze is var-
iable but usually follows the direction of the sun. Starting during the
early morning, it increases in intensity during the day, and at times
reaches a strength of 12 to 16 knots in the afternoon, being strong
enough at this time to present the possibility of interferences with
landing operations for a period of 1 or 2 hours.

ANNEX "ABLE" of OPERATION PLAN
                                       CTF 87 No. 1-44
                                       INTELLIGENCE PLAN

File No.
3Gr8t Phib/A16-3(4)

Serial: 00070   1 August 1944.

TOP SECRET - BIGOT - ANVIL

ANNEX "ABLE" of
OPERATION PLAN
CTF 87 No.1-44.

INTELLIGENCE PLAN

    C. Visibility

        Haze, restricting visibility to 2-5 miles, is very prevalent during
        August and September, mainly from about the beginning of morning twi-
        light until 0800 local time. Occasionally haze has been observed at
        1300, but never at 1800.

        Mirages in the area are frequent and usually take the form of a distort-
        ion of the shoreline.

    D. Tides.

        Normal tides are negligible and rarely run over 6 inches in range. In
        some areas, however, there is a definite change in sea level due to pre-
        vailing winds. Under certain wind conditions, this change in level may
        amount to as much as 2 to 3 feet.

    E. Currents.

        Currents in this area are mostly wind currents and the greatest vel-
        ocities are found along the coast. These coastal currents have a mean
        velocity of about 1 knot, though winds above 25 knots may increase
        this to 2 knots. Eastward of CAP SICIE (near TOULON) the current
        usually sets Westward in response to the prevailing wind, but in the
        GULF OF FEJUS a counter-current setting Eastward is to be expected.
        Along the shore near the harbor of ST. RAPHAEL, a constant current
        sets Northeastward, Eastward and Southeastward, setting out of the bay
        between the islands of LES LIONS.

IV ENEMY DEFENSES AND INSTALLATIONS

    A. Minor Beach Defenses.

        1. The three assault beaches in the CAMEL area are defended in the
           main by pillboxes, casemates and machine gun positions. RED Beach
           (Beach 264A) also has on it an anti-tank wall and ditch and under-
           water obstacles in the form of concrete pyramids, which may be
           mined. In addition, RED Beach and GREEN Beach (Beach 264B) have
           barbed wire on them and are covered by several flat trajectory
           guns.

        2. In general, the casemates and pillboxes differ only in size and in
           the calibre of the guns found in them. The casemates are reported
           to contain guns up to 88 mm., or possibly larger, while the pill-
           boxes probably have nothing above heavy machine guns or light field
           pieces. Both have thick concrete walls and roofs and are designed
           to offer no plane surface to fire.

Page 11 of 16

ANNEX ABLE of OPERATION PLAN
CTF 87 No. 1-44
INTELLIGENCE PLAN

File No.
3Gr8thPhib/A16-3(4)

Serial: 00070   1 August 1944.

TOP SECRET - EYGCT - ANVIL

ANNEX "ABLE" of
OPERATION PLAN
CTF 87 No. 1-44

INTELLIGENCE PLAN

 3. These positions are located directly on RED Beach and on the low,
level ground immediately in back of it. There are about 2 casemates, 13 machine gun positions and 2 anti-tank guns located on RED
Beach and directly behind it. These positions, covering the beach
itself and the logical exits, together with the seawall and road
blocks, form the perimeter of defense of RED Beach.

 4. On GREEN Beach and BLUE Beach (Beach 265A) most of the pillboxes,
casemates and machine gun positions are located on the high ground
to the rear of the beaches and on the rocky extensions on the flanks.
Approximately 7 casemates, 3 of which are still under construction,
6 pillboxes, 2 anti-tank guns and 3 machine guns cover GREEN Beach,
its approaches or the area directly behind and flanking the beach.
About 5 pillboxes and 6 machine gun positions cover BLUE Beach or
the approaches to it.

 5. A complete, detailed list of minor Beach defenses, including a description of them and their respective coordinates, will be found in
Appendix 7, Annex George (Gunfire Support Plan.).

 b. Enemy Coastal Batteries Affecting the CAMEL Area.

It is estimated from photographic reconnaissance and other sources that
there are 56 coastal defense battery positions situated in the Assault
Area. Furthermore there are 10 additional batteries which are out of the
CAMEL Area but fire from which could fall within it. Of the 56 positions
22 were believed to be occupied with a total of 79 individual guns as of
the middle of July. Guns are probably hidden in the vicinity of some of
the unoccupied positions and it is to be expected that artillery will
be moved into certain of the other positions when the enemy becomes
alerted.

Most of the guns in the CAMEL Area are estimated to be light mobile
artillery (75 mm. - 105 mm.) with only 2 or 3 batteries of larger calibre, and they are thought to be 150 mm. or 155 mm. Only one battery
is believed to have casemated gun positions. Others consist of open
emplacements revetted with blocks of rock, sand-bags or earth.

For a list and description of batteries see Appendix 7, to Annex George
(Gunfire Support Plan.)

 c. Underwater Obstacles.

The only underwater obstacles in the area are to be found on RED Beach
where they stretch the entire length of the beach. Concrete pyramids
have been placed from 80 to 420 feet from the waterline to seaward,. The
distance of these obstacles from the beach varies with the gradient,. All
obstacles are in a single irregular row. The greatest distance between
any two obstacles is 18 feet, while the least distance is 6 feet; the
average is 10 feet apart. The pyramids are 5 feet high and 3 feet wide
at the base. On the average their tops are about 1 foot below the surface of the water.

Page 12 of 16   ANNEX ABLE of OPERATION PLAN
                                                    CTF 87 NO. 1-44
                                                    INTELLIGENCE PLAN

File No.
3Gr8thPhib/A16-3(4)

Serial: 00070

1 August 1944.

TOP SECRET - BIGOT - ANVIL

ANNEX "ABLE"of
OPERATION PLAN
CTF 87 No. 1-44

INTELLIGENCE PLAN

    D.   Enemy Order of Battle (Situation as of 20 July 1944)

      Five Infantry Divisions, all but one of which are Limited Employment divisions, hold the entire Southern coast of FRANCE. In addition, one weak Panzer Division, the 9th, located north of NIMES, is the only reinforcing unit in depth along the entire coast. This unit has only 80 medium tanks.

      The calibre of the four Limited Employment divisions is poor, being composed of large numbers of non-Germans. The total strength of each of these divisions, bolstered by all spare regiments and battalions training in the area, will not be more than 8500 men, and the equipment, only partially mobile, is of decidedly inferior quality.

      More than 22,000 MAQUIS, armed by the Allies and fighting in the LYON-GRENOBLE area, have forced the enemy to detach a regiment of the 9th Panzer and a regiment of the 338 Limited Employment Division from the Southern coast, as well as one full division; these units would otherwise be available for reinforcing the coast.

      Divisions are located as follows: Unidentified Field Type, Infantry - NARBONNE; 338th Limited Employment Div. Infantry - ARLE; 244th Limited Employment Infantry - North of AUBAGNE; 242nd Limited Employment Infantry - East of MESSE; 148th Limited Employment Training Infantry - CANNES; 9th Panzer - North of NIMES.

    E.   Enemy Radar

      There are only two known surface warning radar stations in this area and they are situated on either flank of RADE D'AGAY.

      #1. 2 Giant Wurtzburgs (installed Nov. 1943)

         Location: 43° 25' 43" N, 06° 52' 30" E
            grid reference - S-239522.
            on POINTE DE LA BAUMETTE, 5½ miles East of ST. RAPHAEL;
            200 yards inland from the sea.

         Elevation: 96 feet above sea level.

      #2. 1 Wasserman chimney (installed Feb. 1944)

         Location: 43° 25' 00" N, 06° 51' 20" E.
            grid reference - S-222510
            on CAP DE DRAMMONT, 4½ miles east of ST. RAPHAEL;
            200 yards inland from the sea.

         Elevation: 310 feet above sea level.

      For a description and illustrations of these types of radar see page 30 of pamphlet on Enemy Forces, Weapons and Tactics.

Page 13 of 16

ANNEX "ABLE"
INTELLIGENCE PLAN

File No. 3Gr8thPhib/A16-3(4)
Serial: 00070

1 August 1944

TOP SECRET - BIGOT - ANVIL

ANNEX "ABLE" of
OPERATION PLAN
CTF 87 No. 1-44

INTELLIGENCE PLAN

   F. Marine Mines

      Prior to the operation a chartlet will be issued by NCWTF showing
location of minefields reported from various sources and indicating
those whose existence has been confirmed by reconnaissance. Before
radio silence is effective latest mine information for area of operations
will be disseminated by dispatch. For a description of types of Marine
mines see page 26 of pamphlet on Enemy Forces, Weapons and Tactics.

V. COUNTER INTELLIGENCE CAPTURED DOCUMENTS AND EQUIPMENT SECURITY.

   A. Civilian Infiltration of Allied Lines

      1. Civilian personnel -, men, women and children will undoubtedly
attempt to wander among our troops, along the beach and along the
roads and fields in or near our area of operation. Civilian infiltration of our positions must be discouraged. All civilians must be
distrusted. In the past, innocent-seeming civilians wandering among
our troops and along our beach-heads have given the enemy important
information of our activities.

      2. In the event of capture by the enemy, give only NAME, RANK OR RATING
and SERIAL or FILE NUMBER. Commanding officers should make sure that
all personnel understand that in case of capture they are not required
under the Geneva Convention to give any information other than NAME,
RANK or RATING, SERIAL or FILE NO. and that answers to interrogations
should be confined to these items. Prisoner of War Interrogators rel-
ish coming upon those prisoners who are evasive, those who attempt to
deceive or lie, those who brag or boast, those who try to parry wits,
those WHO TALK.

   B. Captured Documents and Equipment.

      1. Every practicable effort will be made to search for and collect enemy
documents from captured or stranded ships, headquarters and Naval
Officers on shore, signal and communication installations, living
quarters, etc. Under no circumstances should captured documents be
destroyed when found. Such documents are the source of information
which may be vital and which, aside from helping to prevent needless
loss of life, may materially affect the course of an operation.

      2. All documents found shall be turned over to the commanding officer of
the unit or his intelligence officer without delay. Effective steps
should be taken to ensure that documents valuable for the information
they may reveal are not thoughtlessly retained by individuals as
souvenirs.

ANNEX "ABLE"
INTELLIGENCE PLAN

File No.
3Gr8thPhib/A16-3(4)

Serial: 00070   1 August 1944.

TOP SECRET-DIGOT-ANVIL

ANNEX "ABLE" of
OPERATION PLAN
CTF 87 No. 1-44

INTELLIGENCE PLAN

3. Documents include: charts, maps, overlays, plans, sketches, direc-
    tives, instructions, operations orders, code and signal books, cell
    lists, dispatches, cipher or code work sheets, logs and records,
    files and correspondence, technical manuals, instruction books, news-
    papers and periodicals, miscellaneous papers of all kinds including
    letters and memoranda, uniform insignia. No document should be re-
    jected because it is partly burned, as an attempt by the enemy to
    burn may be indicative of a documents intelligence value.

4. Captured documents shall be marked with the name of the unit making
    capture or discovery and with the date and place.

5. Document's taken from a prisoner shall be plainly marked with the name
    and serial number of the prisoner and all such documents shall be
    transferred with the prisoner. in order that they be available to
    trained interrogators at subsequent interrogration.

6. Unit commanders shall, when practicable, extract information of
    immediate intelligence value and disseminate to commanders concerned.
    Documents appearing to contain information of immediate interest to
    the Army or Air Forces shall be turned over to the nearest command
    post of those services without delay. To facilitate this exchange
    of documents and information, intelligence liaison will be maintained
    with Army and Air Force commands present.

7. Documents not lending themselves to analysis or evaluation at unit
    level shall be transmitted to the Naval Task Force Commander for
    disposition in accordance with theatre directives.

8. Captured equipment of possible intelligence value shall be reported -
    or if small in bulk and weight transmitted to - the Naval Task Force
    Commander who will direct its disposition. Care shall be taken to
    prevent stripping of small parts or other vandalism which will tend
    to destroy the usefulness of the equipment found or captured.

C. Security

1. Personnel exposed to capture shall not carry any personal papers,
    letters or any other article which might contain information of
    value to the enemy. It is contrary to existing directives to keep
    personal diaries. Commanding Officers may desire to cause search of
    persons, effects, and quarters of personnel to make sure that this
    provision is carried out. Insignia of rank shall not be directly
    visible.

2. No leave or liberty shall be allowed from escort, support or landing
    craft after personnel have been briefed. In cases of sickness or
    other casualty among briefed personnel requiring removal of the
    patient to shore, the hospital is to be warned that the patient has
    been briefed. Ambulance drivers shall be told not to converse with
    the patient.

Page 15 of 16.
                                              ANNEX "ABLE"
                                              INTELLIGENCE PLAN

File No.
3Gr8thPhib/A16-3(4)

Serial: 00070   31 August 1944.

TOP SECRET - BIGOT - ANVIL

ANNEX "ABLE" of
OPERATION PLAN
CTE 87 No. 1-44

INTELLIGENCE PLAN

    3. Working parties for loading of supplies and water or for making repairs shall be escorted and under constant supervision to make sure that no unofficial communication takes place. Guards shall be placed over such working parties while they are aboard.

    4. Every ship and craft shall make special arrangements for the immediate destruction of documents, orders, etc., if capture appears imminent.

    5. No charts, orders, or documents shall be taken on the operation other than those that are absolutely essential to the operation.

    6. Any leakage of information shall be reported to the Task Force Commander immediately.

                                      D. P. MOON
                               Rear Admiral, U.S.N.
           Commander Group 3, 8th Amphibious Force

APPENDICES
      I. Astronomical Tables
      II. Report Plan

DISTRIBUTION
(See special distribution list)

AUTHENTICATED:

THOMAS M. HAMILTON
Flag Secretary

Page 16 of 16   ANNEX "ABLE"
                                               INTELLIGENCE PLAN

File:
3G8Fhib/A16-3(L)

Serial: 00070   1 August 1944, 1200.

TOP-SECRET-BIGOT-ANVIL.

APPENDIX 1 of ANNEX "ABLE" of
OPERATION PLAN.
CTF 87. No. 1-44.

ASTRONOMICAL DATA
for
43° 25' N., 06° 45' E.
All Times are BAKER (G.C.T. plus 2 hours).

Date	*Beginning Morning Civil T-ilight	Sunrise	Sunset	*Ending Evening Civil T-ilight	Moonrise	Moonset	Phase of Moon
Aug. 1	0550	0623	2057	2130	1824	0300	
2	0551	0624	2056	2129	1925	0352	
3	0552	0625	2054	2127	2020	0452	
4	0553	0626	2053	2126	2108	0602	Full
5	0554	0627	2052	2125	2149	0717	
6	0555	0628	2050	2123	2225	0834	
7	0556	0629	2049	2122	2259	0951	
8	0558	0631	2048	2121	2330	1105	
9	0559	0632	2046	2119		1219	
10	0600	0633	2045	2118	0001	1331	
11	0602	0634	2043	2115	0033	1440	Last Qtr.
12	0603	0635	2042	2114	0106	1547	
13	0604	0636	2041	2113	0144	1650	
14	0605	0637	2040	2112	0227	1748	
15	0606	0638	2038	2110	0315	1840	
16	0607	0639	2036	2108	0408	1925	
17	0608	0640	2035	2107	0505	2004	
18	0610	0642	2033	2105	0603	2038	New
19	0611	0643	2031	2103	0702	2108	
20	0612	0644	2030	2102	0802	2135	
21	0615	0645	2028	2050	0901	2200	
22	0616	0646	2027	2057	0959	2224	
23	0617	0647	2025	2055	1059	2248	
24	0618	0648	2023	2053	1158	2314	
25	0619	0649	2022	2052	1259	2342	
26	0620	0650	2020	2050	1401		First Qtr.
27	0621	0651	2019	2049	1504	0015	
28	0622	0652	2017	2047	1607	0053	
29	0624	0654	2015	2045	1708	0138	
30	0625	0655	2014	2044	1806	0233	
31	0626	0656	2012	2042	1856	0337	
Sept. 1	0628	0657	2010	2039	1940	0449	
2	0629	0658	2008	2037	2019	0605	Full
3	0631	0700	2006	2035	2054	0724	
4	0632	0701	2004	2033	2128	0843	
5	0633	0702	2003	2032	2159	0959	

Page 1 of 2 Pages.   APPENDIX 1 of ANNEX "ABLE" of
                                       OPERATION PLAN CTF 87. No. 4-44.

Ellery Sedgwick, Jr. in the Mediterranean.

INVASION OF
SOUTHERN FRANCE

We stopped in Oran on our way to Naples and there I called up Theo[27] who was in Algiers. The call was effected very simply over military telephone lines, and I had a good chat with her and found her well and full of interest in her job.

We went on to Naples the next day and arrived without incident. There was only about six weeks in which to prepare and rehearse for the invasion of Southern France. We found upon our arrival that the plans were in a very preliminary state, in spite of the extended time which Admiral Hewett[28] and his staff had to prepare them. On the trip down (and largely at the instigation of my fellow officers), I had been appointed executive officer of our section and a large part of my time was spent in planning and

---

[27] Theodora Sedgwick Bond was a younger sister who worked for the OSS during WWII, and later married Brig. Gen. William Ross Bond; the only general killed in combat during the Vietnam War.

[28] Admiral Henry Kent Hewitt was the highly decorated commander of amphibious operations in both North Africa and Southern Europe during World War II. Among other honors, he was awarded both the Army and Navy Distinguished Service Medals for his role in the invasion of North Africa.

coordinating the work of the section, getting together all available information regarding enemy gun batteries along the coast.

Naples was a dirty city with very little attraction. The waterfront—which had formally provided probably the most extensive port facilities in the Mediterranean—was completely destroyed. Great ships were sunk alongside of most of the docks. Some of these, however, had rolled over and provided ramps for the docking ships. Most of the buildings immediately facing the port were destroyed also, but the loading and unloading that went on was probably greater than the port had ever experienced. Most of the streets were cobblestone, narrow and winding, and there was nothing else but military traffic in evidence. The people seemed very poor and dirty, but I saw no evidence of starving. They seemed to be taken care of, in one way or another, by the occupying forces.

Our life was divided between ship and shore. Our office was in a building called "the block house," high up on a block over the harbor. It also housed all the other commands, including Army and Navy, which were to participate in the operation. It was highly desirable to live aboard ship because of various diseases that seemed prevalent. All of our officers who tried to live ashore caught the bug at some time or another, and were laid up, so I went back to the ship each night.

Admiral Deyo,[29] who was commander of our bombardment group at Normandy, was assigned the same job with us for this operation, and he shared our office at the block house. I worked

[29] Vice Admiral Morton Deyo served in both the Atlantic and Pacific Fleets. In the Pacific, he commanded gunfire and covering force for the assault and occupation of Okinawa, for which he was awarded the Navy Distinguished Service Medal.

OPERATION DRAGOON

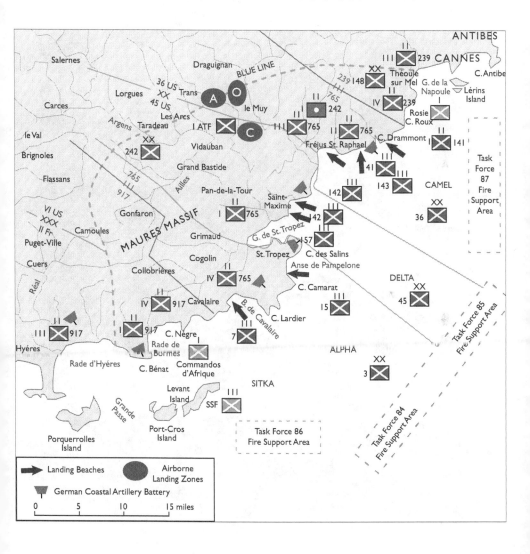

Ellery Sedgwick, Jr. meeting with Dwight D. Eisenhower when he was president.

closely with him and his intelligence officer, Jack Mitchell, in laying out the position of their prospective targets. For graphical visualization of this, we used a rubber model of the terrain that was made up in Norfolk from photographs and maps. It showed all the mountains and hills and was of such a scale as to show each individual house and path. We put colored pins in for the location of the gun batteries and I recall that the Admiral was much impressed with the usefulness of this type of model for planning purposes.

Two young Frenchmen of the French Navy were assigned to work with us. They both came from San Raphael, a town in the center of our objective, and contributed much to our knowledge with such things as landmarks, consistency of the sand and so forth. (They landed with us later and were very useful in contacting local inhabitants to question reliable ones regarding the presence of mines and the whereabouts of the enemy.)

We worked pretty hard those six weeks, but it did not seem to me nearly as hard as preparing for Normandy. For one thing, four weeks before D-Day, our forces in France broke through at St. Lo, and after a huge victory over the enemy at the Falaise Gap, chased him at top speed all across France. He seemed to be staggering and almost on the point of giving up. I personally had many doubts as to whether our operation would ever come off. Another thing that stood out very forcibly there was the very poor security which prevailed. Everyone all through the ranks seemed to be talking about the coming operation and they knew just about where and when it would come off. We were in formerly enemy territory, and we knew he had agents and friends all about. This was an absolute contrast to the secrecy which surrounded the Normandy invasion, when more people had to know the plans. It made us nervous.

The pleasant moments included a jeep ride I took along the Amalfi drive, which was the most beautiful road I had ever been on. It runs between Salerno, 30 miles south of Naples, and just short of Naples along the ocean and along the edge of the great cliffs that drop sharply to the sea. We also visited Pompeii and several times went swimming in the beautiful pool that was used by a group of our hospitals, after having been built originally for a world's fair.

We only held one rehearsal for this operation and that was about eight days before the main show. Last-minute preparations were intense because we were to return from the rehearsal and leave almost immediately for France. There seemed to be a great many important decisions from the high command that were left to the last minute for solutions. As a result, the plans were not worked out with nearly the care or finesse that had been the case for Normandy. The loading of the transports was a bit confusing and not as orderly as it might have been, but all the troops and equipment were on, or very near, the shore which simplified the task. There were three divisions involved in the initial landing—the Third, Fifth, and Thirty-Sixth. Our own group was to carry the latter, a Texas division which had a fair but not outstanding record to date. We were to land these divisions at three separate locations along a fifty-mile stretch of coast. These locations were determined by the suitability of the beach and by the access inland from them to the soft underbelly of the continent. In the early dawn, a few hours before our landing, a division of paratroopers was to be dropped a few miles inland from our beaches which were considered the best defended of them all. The paratroopers were mounted from Sardinia and Corsica. Air support for the entire operation was to come from 12 small carriers under British operation. Long-range bombers from Italy, which had been conducting preliminary strategic bombing for several months, were to prepare the way with heavy tactical bombing just prior to the landing.

In our studies of our landing areas, our best information came from aerial photographs and underground sources in the OSS. We saw a good many defensive positions along the coast, but they were mostly small in size and in no respect compared to those in Normandy. The worst feature we saw was a barrier of underwater obstacles in front of our main assault beach just outside San Raphael. They were concrete pyramids about eight feet high and ten feet apart with their tops just below the surface of the water. They probably had Teller mines attached to them and could prevent any of our assault boats from getting through (as I will develop later).

Our rehearsal proceeded without incident and was on such a limited scale that almost nothing could go wrong. It was primarily an exercise in cruising formation. When we returned to Naples from it, an amazing thing happened. The morning after anchoring, I passed by the Admiral's cabin and saw my friend, Tom Hamilton, come out with a very grave expression. Then I got the word that the Admiral was found dead with a bullet through his head. He had left a very short note saying that it was better for the U.S. Navy that he not conduct any future operations. It was a stunning blow. He was one of the youngest and most promising Admirals. He had a wife and four children and he had a large assault coming up almost immediately. Facts that developed subsequently showed that he had been under tremendous strain for a long time. The staff medical officer had been very concerned about his cracking up and had tried, for most part in vain, to get him to take exercise and some relaxation. He had come to a point where it was tremendously difficult to make a firm decision with speed. He could not differentiate between the minor and major issues. He had started out by finding it almost impossible to delegate responsibility and insisted on knowing everything. In the Mediterranean, he was disturbed about the way in which things were conducted and it was too much for him.

This circumstance was, of course, reported immediately to Vice Admiral Hewitt,[30] commander of the Mediterranean fleet. Admiral Moon[31] was buried ashore in Naples that afternoon. The next morning, Rear Admiral Spencer Lewis,[32] who was the chief of staff to Hewitt, took over command of our force. Of course, he could not hope to know the details of the operation, but he did not hesitate to delegate responsibility and our own chief of staff, Captain Tomkins, made most of the decisions. Lewis had a sense of balance and a sense of humor. (It was indicative of him that, when we returned from this operation, he

[30] Vice Admiral Henry Kent Hewitt was awarded two Army and two Navy Distinguished Service Medals for his service in invading North Africa and Southern France.

[31] Admiral Don P. Moon directed the landings on Utah. Sadly, he committed suicide with his pistol on August 5, 1944. His suicide was attributed to battle fatigue.

[32] Admiral Spencer Lewis commanded the Riviera invasion task force during the Southern France invasion of 1944.

married an attractive British woman, 22 years of age).

I had the opportunity of picking what ship I wanted to go to the area on, so I chose the *Thomas Jefferson*, which was a beautiful converted liner. I had handsome quarters for the short trip, which took us from Naples through the passage between Sardinia and Corsica, and then up to the French coast. I spent much of the time with the men and officers who were to operate the assault boats, and discussed with them the characteristics of the beach, the tides, the currents to be encountered, the landmarks to be used as guides, and the obstacles and defenses to be avoided.

There was not the same tenseness among the men as before Normandy. And while everyone was serious, they did not appear unduly concerned. I instinctively liked the young blonde commander, a fellow of quiet mien, not more than 23 years. He handled men much older than he with entire assurance that came from knowing his business. I made a deal with him to take me in his boat in the morning. I went to bed early that night and slept very soundly with nothing on my mind.

I was almost up too late the next morning for it was 3:30 a.m. when I awoke. We were already coming into position and I dressed hurriedly. After a good breakfast, I went topside to observe the unloading. There was a moderate breeze and quite a current; I could see the ships constantly changing their position to obtain their proper station. To the east, I could hear large numbers of aircraft and I knew they must be the transport planes bringing in paratroopers. But, there were no planes over-head until dawn and our long range bombers came over and dropped their loads on the beaches. Our own assault boats were loaded with troops, which went over the side in very fast time and good order. I believe it took only 22 minutes to get 28 assault boats in the water, even fully loaded with a total of almost 900 troops.

It was about 5 a.m. when I went over the side and down the net to the speed boat that already had been put in the water. We took off in haste for the beach to catch up with the waves that were ahead. As we sped along, the boats repeatedly shook with vibrations from the concussions ashore. Our ships were firing then, the destroyers relatively close in, and the cruisers to seaward firing over them. It was still dark enough to see the red and white shells go overhead and land along the beach. We caught up with the wave of boats and worked our way through the formation.

The first phase of our landing on Red Beach, just to the west of San Raphael, was to be one of the most important and interesting ones. All the waves of assault boats were led by "Apex" boats, or "drone" boats, whose purpose was to blow up the pyramid shaped underwater obstacles that were placed by the enemy about 100 yards off shore at such intervals as to prevent our boats from going between them. These had been carefully noted on aerial photos and we thought they had been provided for by our "drone" boats. The latter were of two types, male and female. The female were filled with about a ton of TNT each and were radio controlled by the male boat which followed several hundred yards after them. The female boats were to be guided to the pyramids and then one charge set off by radio which would sink them, whereupon the second charge would be set off and demolish a pyramid. Everything was fine until they came about 100 yards off shore and then, even as I was watching, the female boats started turning off at weird angles. They began running every which way and going in circles. None of us could conceive of what was happening, but knew something was desperately wrong. Our radio operator soon got the answer. He announced that he had picked up much static and scraps of German on the circuit which governed them. One remark came over the radio which he reported to us as coming through in broken English: *These little boats used to be yours, but they are ours, Yankees.* Indeed they were, except that he could not control them either; the enemy could only interrupt and interfere with our control. It was a good deal lighter now and we could see the boats going crazily about the congested inner harbor. It was apparent that they could not only not accomplish their mission, but would cause great damage to our own forces if the assault was continued.

At this stage, I put on the radio earphones and listened to the reports going through to the command ships. The great question, of course, was: *could the landing go ahead?* There were, I would judge, 10,000 army troops afloat in 400 assault craft on their way to the beach. Could all these be stopped and diverted, and where would they go? I made my report as soon as I could get through on the wire and repeated to the Admiral all the circumstances I saw. I advised that, in my judgment, no landing was practical here.

I believe that within ten minutes the decision was reached on the command ship, and all the assault boats were ordered to proceed, in as close formation as possible, to another beach about five miles distance, and unload there. This other beach, Green Beach, was much smaller, and as a result, not nearly as well protected. A comparatively small force had been assigned to go in there, and had successfully landed in spite of minor interference from the enemy. Before we left the area of Red Beach, we chased and successfully sank, with our 20mm gun, one of the drones that was headed out to sea. The others were scattered all over the bay. A few had run up on the rocks and others were sunk by gunfire. It took several hours to round them all up, but in the meantime, we were on our way to Green Beach trying to assist in leading the waves, which were now out of order though in some assemblance of grouping. There was some slight gunfire from the shore, but it was ineffective and I did not see a boat hit. As we approached Green Beach, we noticed there was some fire coming from a large rock with a tower on it at the entrance to the little bay. Several of our gun boats concentrated on it and it was silenced, but not before at least one casualty within my view occurred.

From then on, the going was fairly easy, the day was uneventful. All beaches were found heavily mined and it took some time to clear them. However, when the afternoon came, we had landed all the troops on the small Green Beach that were originally intended for the much larger Red Beach. When the troops got ashore, they found that most of the enemy had pulled out and left only a relatively small force of mostly foreign troops to guard the entire coast. We found out later that the bulk of the German troops had left four days before, undoubtedly on the basis of a tip and with some knowledge of the overwhelming force that was to land. At the end of three days fighting, our division, the 45th, had less than 300 casualties.

I returned to my ship in the early afternoon and made my full report. In the evening, the German planes came over for the first time and hit at least one of our ships which burned nearly all night. They continued to come at the same time the next few days until we had our own air fields established ashore. It was always one or two light bombers at a time and never in any quantity. The German mining of the beaches and even a good many behind them, as well as other strategic spots, was incredible. On our small Blue Beach, the mines were three layers deep. Sometimes after detecting and pulling up a mine on the top layer, it would set off a mine three feet below with the same deadly effect. Twice they thought the beach was clear but had casualties when they started to unload across it, and upon checking, found even a third layer of Teller mine. The day after the landing, I saw a nasty incident in which two fellows were killed and another badly injured as their jeep ran just off the pavement and into the softer ground at the edge setting off a mine. All this made my job on shore very nerve-wracking, and I remember my sentiments as I went about checking on certain enemy gun positions and encampments. They purposely played on your nerves, too, by putting up big signs reading: "Beware: Mines." In most, but not all of these places, it would be safe.

Two days after the landing, our forces had just reached Cannes, the beautiful resort spot. We had a mission to find out from the local fisherman and French authorities what sea areas were mined, so that our ships could effectively support the movement of our troops along the shore. We put our jeep ashore at St. Raphael and entered Cannes just as our troops were clearing the fleeing Germans from it.

There were still a good many roadblocks (undefended) and blown bridges, but still the drive along the shore was lovely, except when you occasionally came across the bodies of dead Germans who had not moved quite fast enough. When we first got in the city, everything was very quiet, except for an occasional shooting. All the French were in their cellars, but when the air cleared a little and they saw us walking about, they came back out and opened up their doors and stores as usual. Great crowds formed about us to ask the news and to offer us everything that was theirs. The Maquis began forming together in bands and with all kinds of weapons on them from shotguns to pistols, and asked us about the enemy. We contacted the Mayor and the harbor master who called in all the leading fishermen, and from their accounts, prepared charts of the harbor areas and where the sea mine fields were. Then, we got guides to take us to the former German command headquarters, which was in a beautiful house and grounds formerly owned by some New York Wall Streeter. It had been a magnificent place knocked badly by our naval bombardment and was left in great haste. We found rather crude booby traps there, but also some documents of interest and value. The caretaker of the place was still in the cellar when we arrived.

Back in town again, all the doors were open to us and everyone begged us to come in and have a drink. They opened their best champagne and in one restaurant we stopped at, an orchestra appeared and played the Star Spangled Banner and the Marseilles alternately. The crowds almost went crazy and I think that I could honestly say that there was hardly a soul who wasn't crying his eyes out with the emotion of it.

The people were all very underfed, but aside from this, they had not been harshly treated, unless they were definitely unsympathetic to the Germans (in which event, the younger men were taken off to work). We had brought with us a good many K rations and we passed the food out particularly to the kids who were ravenous for it. That was a pathetic and sad scene. Probably the scene that touched me most was an old man with the customary beard who pushed his way through the crowd and took me by the hand. He held it with both of his and said, "Vous êtes arrivés." My imperfect ear caught his gratefulness and the fact that he had hoped for this day when the Americans would come and he would be happily free. His eyes were streaming tears, but they sparkled like lights.

Our ship stayed off Southern France for about five weeks and it was a pleasant time for us all. I went ashore almost every day and we picked out a wonderful beach to sun at—after the mines were cleared. The water was delicious and the air was the most refreshing in the world. It is soft and scented with the pines. This was the life. We had not enjoyed such a quiet, restful experience for many months, and we took full advantage of it. The only intelligence work to be done was to make up detailed reports on the principal enemy methods of defense which included their network of mine fields, ashore and off shore, and their interlocking strong points and coastal batteries protecting the shore line. These reports were rather good fun to compile after the initial work of collecting the data was completed. There were invariably booby traps of one kind or another about the defenses which had been set by the fleeing Germans. One had to move about with the greatest caution, and with your heart in your mouth. To illustrate the reports, we added some excellent photographs and sketches drawn by Turkette, and they made a good showing as they went in to the higher command.

As the days went by, the conversation focused more and more on what the next step for us was. We were hoping to go back to the States, quite naturally, and that was the probability. There was a lot of talk, however, about helping the British with an operation in the Eastern Mediterranean. Finally, we got the signal to go back to Naples to report again to Admiral Hewitt for further assignment. When we arrived, the word went around that we would sit here for some time before the brass hats figured out what to do with us. So on the second or third evening of our stay, I was invited to stay ashore with a friend of mine who lived there, and did so. We spent the evening at a couple of officer's clubs and went to bed about midnight. About 4 a.m., a friend, Harry Midgely, came bursting in and shook me until I was on my feet. He hurried me into my uniform and down to the dock where a boat was waiting to take us to our ship. Harry had been ashore that evening and when he returned to the ship at midnight, he had heard the news that we were to leave at 6 a.m. in the morning for the United States. He knew I was ashore but did not know who with or where. Starting from scratch and with the greatest determination, he found out at this late hour who I was with and where he lived. It was a remarkable feat, and if it were not for Harry's efforts, I would have been left in Naples.

We were in excellent humor on our journey home. We knew we were headed for the Pacific, but at least we would be home again for a short while, and that was worth anything. I can only remember two incidents on that homeward journey. The first was going through the Straits of Gibraltar when our little convoy was lit up by the strong search lights from Spanish Tangiers. There was no reason for it except to provide the German agents there with information on allied ship movements. It made me very angry. The second was when a few hundred miles off the

U.S. coast, our convoy split, part of it headed to New York and we headed for Norfolk. Just as the New York section was pulling out of site, it flashed a message: "Will join up with you again at the Astor bar." One of the more serious-minded staff officers had the bridge at the time. He had the quartermaster break out all the charts of that part of the coast, but he could find no Astor bar.

What a tremendous thrill it was to get home again. It was early October 1944. I was lucky enough to get a plane out of that hellhole Norfolk, which took me directly to Cleveland, to my wife and babies. It was my first view of Irene, now six months. It was night when I arrived home at the cottage at Valley Ridge,[33] and little Irene was in her crib upstairs. When she opened her eyes and saw me she raised up her arms to me and from then on I was pretty much sold. We had three wonderful weeks together and then back to Norfolk I went. But only overnight, for I got an additional few days leave, and at the end of these, I took Sis and Irene to Washington in the hope that I could persuade the authorities to let me do a little intelligence research there before the ship sailed. It worked well and we spent another week together at Net's house in Georgetown. The parting was very sad when I finally had to go. The Pacific War seemed interminable, but I felt pretty sure about getting back by Christmas of 1946.

When we arrived in the States, we were a staff without an Admiral or command, so there was much speculation as to whom we would be attached and what our first job would be.

---

[33] Valley Ridge was a farm in Gates Mills, Ohio; owned by Ellery's wife's family.

We soon learned that we would go to Rear Admiral Kiland,[34] newly appointed to that rank and given command of the amphibious group serving under Admiral Turner[35] in the Pacific. He had flown to Pearl Harbor ahead of us and we were to follow by ship and join him. Furthermore, we were to have a new flag ship, but the *Bayfield*, which we had been on since Plymouth, was to take us to Pearl Harbor. The stack itself was changed and cut down a bit before we left the States. Bob Thayer was doing everything in his power to get off, but only got a promise to be let off after the next operation. Our section was cut nearly in half. Only Parrish, Burwell, Turkette, McGowen, Dalton, and myself remained.

[34] Rear Admiral Ingolf Norman Kiland was awarded the Navy Cross for his courage commanding the amphibious force during the Battle of Guadalcanal in November 1942. He retired as Vice Admiral in April 1957.

[35] Admiral Richmond K. Turner held various amphibious force commands in the Pacific as rear admiral and vice admiral. He prophetically predicted in 1940 that the next Japanese aggression would bring the U.S. and Japanese to war.

SOUTH PACIFIC & OKINAWA

We left the morning I arrived in Norfolk and our first stop of interest was Panama. To our immense disappointment, we were only scheduled to stop there a few hours and no one was to be let ashore. However, a special invitation came for me from John Goren, my old friend from Panama days, to take lunch with him and bring along a couple of friends. He would send his launch over. In as much as he was Port Director, permission was granted, and with everyone else on the ship scowling at us, off we went. We had a wonderful time seeing my old friends, buying presents for our wives, and just sitting over excellent drinks. My friend John Ives was on hand and had our transportation all arranged. Almost all of my old friends had left, of course, but I saw Hugh Dabney, and a few others. We had a good lunch at the Tivoli with the two Johns, and then a stop at Mota's to buy alligator bags and silk stockings for sending home.

The next stop, after about a week, was our arrival at Pearl Harbor. It was my first view of it. The harbor is hard to recognize as you approach because there are no high hills around it and part of it is artificial. Still the island looked pretty good to us, and the air was marvelous.

Our ship, the good old *Bayfield*, was taken away from us very promptly and we had to move ashore. Our stay lasted all too short a time. Rumor had it that we were originally scheduled for the Iwo Jima operation, which was still a good five months ahead and would have given us good time for preparation. But, another Admiral and his staff flying west had been lost over the ocean and we were to now be substituted for him. Admiral Kiland, Thayer, and a few others, had already left by plane to some un-identified spot. We had two hectic days in Hawaii getting maps, charts, other intelligence material, and then 12 of us took off by plane. The rest, some 50 odd, were to follow shortly by ship.

Those plane trips were mighty uncomfortable. One has only the aluminum bucket seat to sit on with no back and, if you are lucky, you can crawl up on the hard deck of the plane. The best part of that trip was the coffee and donuts the Red Cross girls gave us before we started. The first stop was Johnston Island about 800 miles out, a tiny speck with a coral reef around it and hardly long enough to land a large plane. There was not a stick of shrubbery, only sand, and I had great sympathy for the 200 odd souls there who had to spend months and even years in the one spot. We next came down in Kwajalein Atoll[36] for gas and a bit of food. I can't say that I was very enthusiastic about it. Our last stop in the plane was Guadalcanal, Henderson Field.

---

[36] Kwajalein Atoll is in the Marshall Islands, in the central Pacific Ocean, between Hawaii and the Philippines.

GUADALCANAL

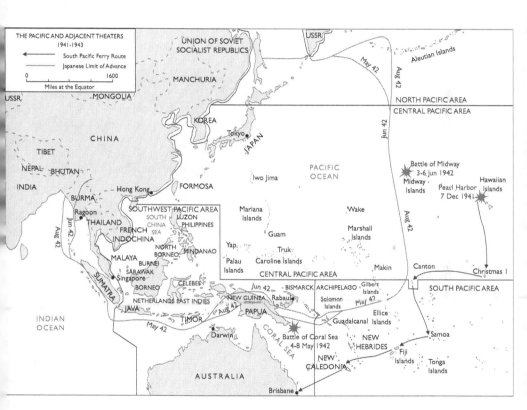

NEW GUINEA

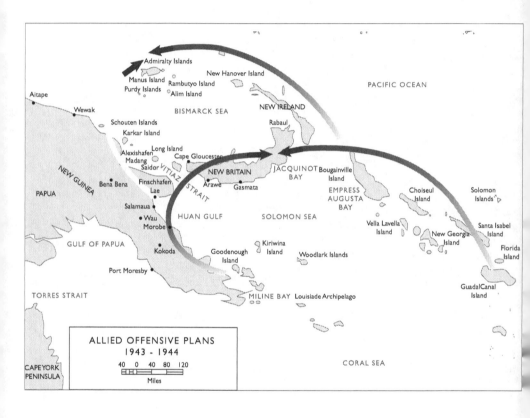

ALLIED OFFENSIVE PLANS
1943 - 1944

40   0   40   80   120

Miles

Here we got a bite of breakfast from the Red Cross girls and finally ended up at Hotel Digink for a wash down and rest. This was an outrageous excuse for a traveler's stop, consisting of canvas cots in a large open tent enclosed by netting. There was little running water. No one on the island had ever heard of our Admiral and it took most of the day chasing about to get a lead as to where he might be and how to reach him. Finally, by splitting up, we got space in a smaller plane going to Bougainville.[37]

It was an interesting trip up the chain of Solomon Islands, over many small tropical mountainous islands, past the hulk of Japanese ships which had been apprehended in trying to bring in reinforcements. It was a journey over mostly enemy held territory. Even on Bougainville, we held only a seven-mile area on the whole island, but it turned out to be a very pleasant little spot with excellent facilities considering its advanced location. We did find the Admiral there, and I saw Thayer for the first time in two months.

Bougainville was a fine place to do our planning, or at least that seven-mile perimeter that was ours and not the Japanese. It was very green and lush with the high hills and a couple volcanoes behind. The encampment was well-built with an excellent central dining hall and an attractive little officer's club where we could get two cans of beer a day. We slept in little wooden huts at first, but then moved to comfortable Quonset huts. The heat was quite intense, but within the fortnight we had an air conditioned hut for an office. There were a number of relatively tame parakeets that came around for food, and flowers were abundant.

---

[37] Bougainville is a part of Papau New Guinea.

I soon found out that we were to be part of Vice Admiral Wilkinson's[38] force going in on the critical landing at Lingayen Gulf on Luzon, which was to be the second major landing in the Philippines. Our groups were lifting the 37th division (Ohio's own) commanded by Major General Beightler.[39] From the Intelligence standpoint, there was not a great deal that we could accomplish by way of preparation—because we had almost no information. The only hydrographic survey we had was over 40 years old, and considering the tides and surf in the area, we could not place much confidence in them, the gradient, the depths, etc. Furthermore, the only aerial photos that had been taken to date were from very high altitude and gave very little detail of value. The only other information came through devious channels from friendly natives who had been contacted by our patrols, but subsequently proved to be quite unreliable. I do not blame this on our informant, but rather on the channels of transmission and the scope of the individual analysis.

One of my jobs during this period was to keep a plot of the disposition of all of the important units in the Japanese fleet. We received almost daily dispatches giving very complete and accurate information on this vital matter. The source of this information was, in large part, sightings by our own search and

[38] Vice Admiral Theodore "Ping" Wilkinson was appointed director of the Office of Naval Intelligence in October 1941. Then he became Deputy Commander, South Pacific, under Admiral William Halsey and Gen. Douglas MacArthur. He is credited with the successful "leapfrogging" strategy whereby the Americans would attack positions behind Japanese forward outposts and cut their supply lines. He died tragically in February 1946 in a ferry accident at Hampton Roads in which he saved his wife's life, but lost his own.

[39] Major Gen. Robert Sprague Beightler commanded the 37th Infantry "Buckeye" Division. Hailing from Sedgwick's home state of Ohio, Beightler the only National Guard General to command his division for the entire length of the war.

reconnaissance planes, and for the rest, radio intelligence.

Let me repeat here that one: the most important job of an amphibious intelligence section is the planning stage of an operation. It is to provide accurate and complete information regarding the landing beaches and the approaches there to. Landmarks to guide boats in, as well as gradient, surf conditions etc., are all of vital importance to the landing boat area, as well as the commanders who make the decisions. We did the best we could with our scant information and Turkette did a good job reconstructing an oblique view of the beach solely on the basis of photographs.

As I have mentioned, the officer's club at Bougainville was an excellent one, even though they also experienced the ever present shortages. We slept comfortably in spite of the heat in raised Quonset huts.

It was in Bougainville that I first met Admiral Kiland, who had flown ahead of us with Thayer, and others. He was, at that time, quiet and pleasant and feeling his way. He was a new Admiral and obviously wanted favorable regard from his officers. I was quite well impressed.

Shortly after the ships came in bringing the rest of our fellows from Pearl Harbor (the ones who would not come with me by air), we shoved off for our first and only rehearsal of the landing. Our troops, the 37th division (Ohio's own), commanded by Major General Beightler, were assembled from the Solomon's area. After a couple of days of sailing we all rendezvoused Lae and Solomon off New Guinea. For sometime we had been promised our flag ship, the *Mt. McKinley*, but she was being used off of Leyte by McArthur forces and was not to be released till the last minute. Therefore, our command was split up on several ships. It was impossible to do any work. I remember reading most of the time and writing home.

Just before we arrived at Lae, I got a signal that the Admiral wanted me aboard his ship, so I transferred over. I was pleased at the compliment, but dismayed when I saw my quarters. There were about 18 of us jammed into a tiny deck house raised on the afterdeck the size of an ordinary bunk cabin. The heat was greater than I have ever felt before or since. I do not know how anyone stood it. I managed to get a cot and slept on the open deck. Those who were forced to sleep below were much worse off.

Thayer was off at this time on an expedition to Hollandia to try to collect more information, so I was assembling and evaluating intelligence for the Admiral. There was not much of significance coming in, but I did track known Japanese subs and plotted enemy planes from whatever dispatch we received.

The exercises went off reasonably well, but were very brief because we had to get on to Manus[40] and assemble there for the main operation. It was a striking harbor. A huge lagoon with a lot of shipping, much of it there for repair, in the huge floating dry dock that had been towed from the States. It was in Manus that we spent Christmas of '44, and it was the dreariest one I've had before, or since. It was hot as hinges and our group was widely scattered on several ships. The only alleviating fact was that there was a heavy delivery of mail that morning and almost everyone got at least one to ten letters from home. They certainly meant an awful lot to all of us. There was a big officer's club on

[40] Manus Island is a part of northern Papau New Guinea.

Manus and most of the fellows went in for little celebration, but I stayed on board. In Manus, I ran into my old boss in Panama, Forest Tucker. He seemed to be doing a good job. He was now a captain. Our flag ship was finally delivered to us there and it was, indeed, a relief to get into our new quarters. The *Mt. McKinley,* as other ships of her type, was designed to carry command of both Army and Navy in an amphibious operation. Her principal feature was the very extensive radio and radar facilities. You could receive and send messages on a great number of channels and control about 25-30 planes in the air, being in direct communication with each at the same time. The Intelligence Office was a thing of beauty to us. It was air-conditioned and had all kinds of room for charts, plots, reference material, and so forth. The only damper on our feelings was when our following luggage, which I had last seen in Pearl Harbor, arrived on board. It had evidently sat out in the sun for days and days because I had many clothes ruined. We also had the Army on board with us, which made it a bit crowded, but still it was heaven when compared to what we had been used to.

As we weighed anchor for Lingayen,[41] we all had some misgivings, principally from our knowledge of Japanese air power which we knew was still far from eliminated in the Philippines. Also, our route took us through the very narrow Straits of Surigao where the Japanese could not fail to observe us and prepare. The only ships to go through these Straits a few weeks before had very heavy going over and several were lost. Our first call to General Quarters was about noon following the night we

---

[41] Lingayen is a municipality in the Philippines.

went through the Straits, and they became more frequent during the afternoon and evening as we went north along the coast. Our convoy, which included some eight transports (ATs) and four cargo ships (AKs), was escorted by four destroyers, two destroyer escorts, and two escort carriers. The latter were the object of most of the attacks, but the transports were not overlooked entirely. It was my first eyewitness experience with Kamikaze or suicide attacks by the Japanese. They had begun this tactic at Leyte Gulf a few months before and it was to reach its climax at Okinawa where we experienced it steadily for over 60 days.

Our air cover was effective in keeping large groups of Japanese planes from coming in close to the convoy, but there were a good many single Japanese planes that got through. One in particular I can never forget. A group of us were sitting in chairs on the deck outside of the General's cabin. We were relaxed and chatting when a plane appeared on the horizon. Several of the experts in plane recognition identified it as a new type of U.S. carrier plane. It was coming in at high speed, only a few yards over the water, directly for us. When only a short ways of, it lifted up to clear us. It was then that we saw the big red Japanese moon under the wings. There was a mad scramble for the General's cabin door and six of us tried to get through it at once. The General, needless to say, could not figure what occasioned this sudden visitation until he heard the alarm a second later. I do not know why this pilot did not choose to hit us because we also did not fire a shot. He went on over the convoy and was shot down by AA fire on his way back.

LINGAYEN GULF

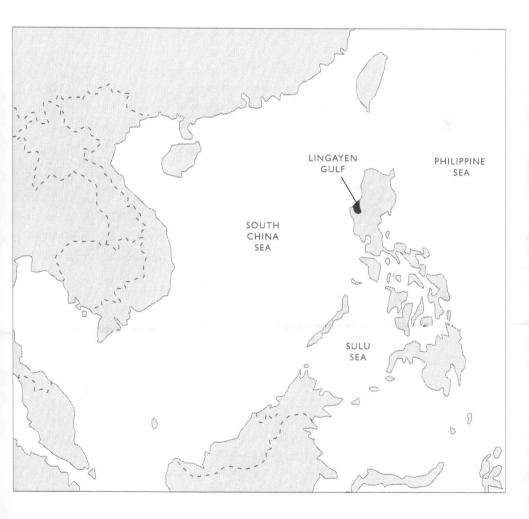

Ellery Sedgwick, Jr. (seated bottom right) briefing fellow officers.

Ellery Sedgwick, Jr. (center) in the Mediterranean, August 18, 1944.

Lt. Commander Sedgwick, Jr. in New York City, NY for training in 1942.
To his right are his wife Elizabeth (Sis), and their oldest son, Ellery Sedgwick III.

Ellery Sedgwick's brother-in-law Brig. Gen. William Ross Bond, was the only general killed in combat in Vietnam. He was married to Sedgwick's sister, Theodora.

Gen. Sedgwick, a collateral ancestor of Lt. Commander Sedgwick, served as the Sixth Corps commander during the Civil War. He was the highest-ranking Union Army officer killed during the war, when a sharpshooter shot him at Spotsylvania Courthouse in 1864.

A short while later, another Japanese aircraft came directly over us almost hitting the mast, but he was followed closely by the two planes who shot him down on our port beam. If my memory serves me right, one cargo ship was hit badly and had to drop astern with a DE escort. The most tragic sight, however, came before dark. Just as the carriers were to take back their last patrols, one of them was hit by a suicide plane and listed badly. Her planes circled her as the darkness came on, but fire had broken out and she finally had to be abandoned. Some of her planes were taken on the other carriers in the end, but I think some had to be ditched and the pilots picked up.

There followed a reasonably quiet night without undo excitement. I had a good sleep, but I was up early for it was January 7th, the day of the Lingayen landing. It was a clear morning with a good many Japanese planes flying at high altitudes. Our AA had a hard time reaching them, as I remember no hits in the landing area even though the sky was filled with streamers from the 20mm guns and bursting shells from the 5-inch guns. It was well to keep under cover and keep one's helmet on because much of the fire was almost directly over head, expending bullets and shrapnel. I remember seeing only one Japanese suicide dive which was successful, but the record will show that a good many of our ships were hit, some two, three, or even four times by individual planes. Fortunately for us, the Japanese at this time were concentrating their efforts on our war ships, which were less vulnerable than the transports and ships such as our command ship. For the most part, the war ships were on the outskirts of the armada and therefore the attacks not directly witnessed by us.

Aside from their air activity, the enemy made virtually no attempt to stop our landing. In complete order and on schedule, all our assault craft were lowered, and went into the designated beaches on the southern shore of the gulf and just north of the little town of Bumaley. Some difficulty was reported as the result of the high surf that was running which proved to be a more serious obstacle the following day when supplies were being moved to shore. The entire landing was effected, of course, after a heavy saturation of the beaches and the shore area by bombardment of shells and rockets. The only casualties of this preparation, as we subsequently learned, were about 200 Filipinos and many cattle and water buffalo.

I do not recall it as a particularly exciting day for me, like my previous two landings. I was on board the *Mt. McKinley* all the time, standing the routine watches and keeping plots from reports of our movement ashore. The aerial activity subsided as soon as the sun was up and our own air cover from light carriers was up. We saw almost no Japanese planes between 10 a.m. and dark. The Commanding General went ashore early in the afternoon which indicated that all our positions were secured.

One incident that produced comments later was the decoration by MacArthur of one of his Generals four days later. The General was awarded with the distinguished service cross for his capture of the enemy air strip near the beaches. Not one shot was fired and it was a perfectly routine maneuver.

Let me inject here with one little sidelight that occurred several days before. As our convoy was approaching the Philippines, we tuned in on the wardroom radio to Tokyo Rose in Japanese. In a quite pleasant voice, she talked along about our present effort, giving quite accurate details as to where we were at the moment and what the composition of our task force was. She offered her heartfelt sympathy to all those young Americans who were proceeding to Japanese territory to meet their doom. She pictured the Japanese as being entirely ready and eager to meet us. I do not think the Japanese knew our landing spot, but they evidently did know much of our movement. In the evening of the day of our landing, Japanese planes were in the air above us; but as I recall, the night was especially dark and they did not inflict serious damage.

Let me go back a moment to another significant military episode. Admiral Oldendorf [42] was in charge of the two-day preliminary bombardment of the beaches. He had command of the old battleships and cruisers which were regularly used throughout the Pacific War for this purpose. The Japanese planes had been hammering at his force on their approach, and after his first day of beach bombardment (which I mentioned was a completely wasted effort), he sent his dispatch to Admiral Halsey [43] who was then commanding the Third Fleet which was attacking air fields and shipping around Luzon. He also sent word to Nimitz, [44] saying, in effect, that the whole landing was precarious

---

[42] Admiral Jesse B. "Oley" Oldendorf won the Navy Cross for sinking two Japanese battleships and preventing the Japanese from entering the Surigao Strait and attacking the beachheads on Leyte Island. He was promoted to vice admiral and named commander of Battleship Squadron 1. He commanded the battleships in the landings at Lingayen.

[43] Fleet Admiral William "Bull" Halsey Jr. was one of four officers to attain the rank of fleet admiral of the Navy. In 1943 he was named commander of the Third Fleet, a post he held until the end of the war. In that role he commanded campaigns from the Philippines to Japanese.

[44] Fleet Admiral Chester Nimitz was Commander in Chief, U.S. Pacific Fleet and Commander in Chief, Pacific Ocean Areas. A fleet admiral wears five stars and Nimitz was one of only four along with Admirals Halsey, Bill Leahy and Ernest King.

because his force had been heavily hit, practically disabled, and, if the Japanese air defenses kept up, it might be disastrous. We saw this message, of course, because N2 intelligence received copies of all dispatches. It did not cheer us up. Poor Oldendorf was, I think, quite bitterly attacked by the regular Navy people of rank for this frank expression of his opinion. The gist of their comment was that "Oley" was probably getting too old and couldn't take it. It seemed to me a foolish reaction, a rather blind respect for courage, regardless of the other issues involved. I forget the exact reply he got, but the inference was to go ahead with the job and forget his casualties. Fortunately, the Japanese air effort did subside, or did appear to, partly because with the arrival of the whole force there were more targets. Their air effort seemed to subside primarily, I think, because of Halsey's carriers pounding Japanese air bases, not only in Luzon, but also in Formosa. They were the only light carriers covering the target area at least in the day time.

On the day after the landing, I was sent ashore with one or two other intelligence officers to contact the Army and learn of their disposition and contacts with the enemy. We first examined the beaches and there was no evidence of enemy fortification. The only defense we could observe was the destruction of several bridges on the roads going south. To be sure, there were some damaged buildings and dead animals around, but they were the result of our own bombardment. I contacted the Army G2 as rapidly as possible and found that no opposition was being encountered, except small groups of Japanese some 15 miles south and artillery forces of considerable strength on the left (east) flank. Artillery continued to shell our flank positions and our ships for some two weeks. None of us, however, knew what to make of the lack of real evidence of the enemy, and we were fearful of an ambush which never occurred. When my immediate job was done, we did a little sightseeing about the village of Dagupan. The Filipinos all appeared to be very friendly and were cordial and smiling, but the countryside was pretty well stripped by the Japanese and these people had little left in the way of possessions.

On the way back to the ship, we had a couple of mishaps, but not because of the enemy. In the first place, a jeep in which we were hitchhiking rolled over going down a bed road and threw us out, or rather we leaped when we saw what was happening. There were a couple slight injuries; nothing serious. Then, when we came to the shore, there was quite a heavy sea running, and we found that a great deal of difficulty had been encountered during the day in bringing supplies ashore. It had become worse in the evening, and nothing could move in. A good many craft were strewn along the beach and could not be put out again. We took one of the last boats to get off an LCT and I remember the pounding was so great it knocked down the bow, and we shipped a lot of water. I was mighty glad to have a life preserver with me. This high surf proved to be the principal problem the next day, and supplies did not start to move smoothly ashore until we made a survey of the river, which emptied into the gulf within the beach area, of which we had assumed to be too shallow for our boats. A survey showed there was a channel at most stages of the tide though, and this simplified unloading problems enormously.

One other incident worth recording was that on the first night or two, there was severe damage done to our ships by unknown enemy craft. They had sneaked up in the darkness and dropped depth charges near the hulls of our ships and raced away. We ascertained that there was a sizable fleet of these boats hidden in a nearby cove, well-camouflaged during the day. These were heavily bombed and shelled, and thus surrounding waters were more thoroughly patrolled on subsequent nights. At this time, our Intelligence section could only get a limited description of these craft. None were captured until quite a while later. The operator of one boat that had met with a mishap was recovered from the water and brought aboard another ship wherein he was questioned by our Japanese Language Officer, who gained some information regarding speed and maneuverability from him.

We remained in the operating area about six days before getting orders to return to Leyte. Incidentally, on this operation, we were one of the two amphibious groups (the other commanded by Rear Admiral Royal) both under the command of Vice Admiral Wilkinson.[45] I sat in on several of his daily staff meetings and was much impressed by his reasonable way of handling things. I think he had unusual capacity and was always very considerate of us. (He met an untimely death just after the war when his auto rolled off a Norfolk ferry boat. He pulled his wife out, but he went down.) I remember that, as usual, we were very thrilled to get our orders to leave. The Japanese air attacks were far fewer on subsequent days than on the first day, but still, it was a good deal healthier elsewhere. The troops moved south toward Manila

---

[45] See footnote 37.

and we were soon out of touch with them. The Intelligence job became quite inactive. The only key function was to provide for the proper unloading of follow-up supplies and troops.

Our trip back was uneventful, except as we drew abreast of the Japanese airfields around Manila. We had several alerts, but no attackers came through to threaten any of the convoy. We spent most of the few days basking on deck, playing hand ball, and speculating on what our next assignment was to be.

Our orders took us to Leyte[46] and when we arrived there, we were not overly enthusiastic regarding our fortune. Our ship, the *McKinley,* was taken away and we were given about 12 hours to move all our gear to another ship. The Naval establishment at Leyte was very primitive, and as one moved about on shore, one only got the impression of masses of mud. It differed from any other mud I had ever encountered in its ability to suck you down and ooze about your feet and legs.

We were soon on our way to Ulithi[47] which was to be our planning base for the next operation, for there was not time to send us back to Pearl Harbor. Ulithi was the first set of coral islands I had ever seen. It is a chain of atolls in the form of a bracelet, thirty miles long and 15 miles wide in the southwest Pacific, about 600 miles from the nearest land. It was a great anchorage for our fleet during our last two years of the war, and almost every Navy ship on active duty out there came in at some time or other for fuel, repairs, shells, or other logistics. It was, however, a poor place for recreation with almost no facilities. When

---

[46] Leyte is an island in the Visayas group of islands in the Philippines.

[47] Ulithi is an atoll in the Caroline Islands of the western Pacific Ocean.

we arrived, the Admiral and a few of his staff were given quite comfortable quarters on a repair ship while the rest of us went to tents at a very nice little base on the beach.

Bob Thayer went back to Pearl by air to get the latest intelligence on our next objective, which we now learned would be Kerama Retto, Okinawa Gunto. Bob had been promised release after the Lingayen Operation and I judged he pulled all wires possible while in Pearl to make this effective, which it eventually was in about a month's time. So from that time on, I was in charge of the N2 till the end.

I used to go ashore almost every day and work with the fellows in the preparation of our Intelligence Plan and the accumulation of data. In the evening, there was often a chance for a swim in the delicious clear water. One had to watch out very carefully for the very sharp coral rocks—or best of all, wear old sneakers. There was a little officer's club here which they opened for us each day for half an hour, and it made a lot of difference. It was here that I ran into Del Marting from Cleveland, who was on the Admiral's Staff in command of a battleship division. He asked me out, and I had an exceedingly pleasant evening having supper with the Admiral, and inspecting the great, new *Iowa,* about which I had heard so much about. Also, while in Ulithi, I heard with great shock that the cruiser *Ticonderoga* had been hit. I knew that George Merriweather, at whose home I had lived in Cleveland for three years, was aboard her. When the news came in that she was coming into our harbor, I arranged for a boat and went over. Much to my relief, I found him in very good shape, but the ship had been hit by a kamikaze and had to return to the States for repair.

THE PHILIPPINES

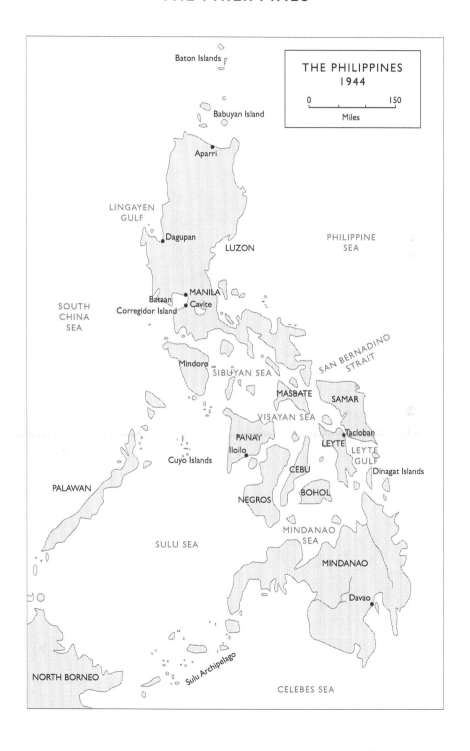

Baton Islands

THE PHILIPPINES
1944

0   150

Miles

Babuyan Island

Aparri

LINGAYEN
GULF

Dagupan

LUZON

PHILIPPINE
SEA

SOUTH
CHINA
SEA

Bataan   MANILA
Corregidor Island   Cavite

Mindoro

SIBUYAN SEA

SAN BERNADINO
STRAIT

MASBATE

SAMAR

VISAYAN SEA

PANA'I

Iloilo

Cuyo Islands

Tacloban

LEYTE

LEYTE
GULF

CEBU

Dinagat Islands

PALAWAN

NEGROS

BOHOL

MINDANAO
SEA

SULU SEA

MINDANAO

Davao

NORTH BORNEO

Sulu Archipelago

CELEBES SEA

ULITHI

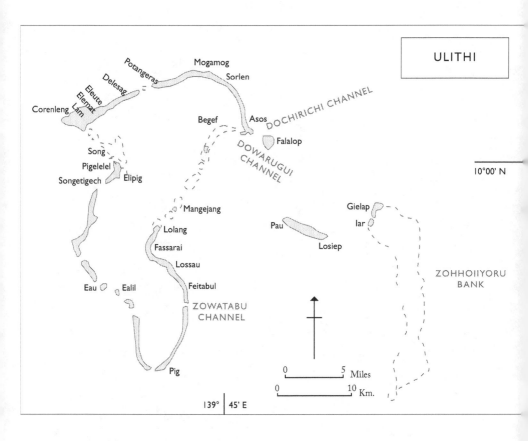

ULITHI

Potangeras

Mogamog

Sorlen

Delesag

Eleute

Elemat

Corenleng   Lam

Begef

Asos

DOCHIRICHI CHANNEL

Falalop

DOWARUGUI CHANNEL

Song

Pigelelel

Songetigech   Elipig

10°00' N

Mangejang

Gielap

Iar

Lolang

Pau

Fassarai

Losiep

Lossau

Eau   Ealil

Feitabul

ZOHHOIIYORU BANK

ZOWATABU CHANNEL

Pig

139°   45' E

0   5   Miles

0   10 Km.

I think we stayed in Ulithi about three weeks studying our assignment. It was not one of the more desirable ones. Our small force, consisting of under a division, were to go into a group of rugged little islands which lay off the main island of Okinawa six days before the main assault force. We were to secure an anchorage and the adjacent islands were to be used as a refueling and reammunitioning base, where ships involved in the primary attack could come. Naturally, our prior information regarding this almost unknown spot was very limited. Some aerial photographs had been taken but they were not good, and we could learn very little about the tides and depths and so forth. We had supposed the islands almost completely uninhabited, but from the photographs we thought we perceived activity. The principal intelligence we had was that missionaries many years before had reported treacherous currents and poisonous snakes.

One thing our section did accomplish at Ulithi was to prepare a little booklet on special Japanese weapons with their use and tactics, which later created considerable interest.

About the middle of February 1945, we moved on again. The Admiral and a few of us left by plane back to Leyte. It was a distance of about 1,000 miles, and it was the first time a plane had made the flight. There was no particular problem to it except that the coral island from which we took off afforded a very short runway for a DC3, and our plane had barely raised from the ground when we were over the water. Even the pilot was a little bit nervous.

At Leyte, we went through about a month of intensive preparation. We eventually got back on board our ship, the *McKinley*, to everyone's relief. This ship afforded not only excellent

KEREMA ISLANDS

Kuroshima

Zamami Island

Gishippu-jima

Zamani

Yakabi Island

Ijakaja Island

Kahi Island

Agenashiku
Island

Amuro-jima

Jo Island

Aka Island

Tokashiki

Geruma Island

Tokashiki Island

Fukaji Island

Kip

Kuba Island

Ojima Islands

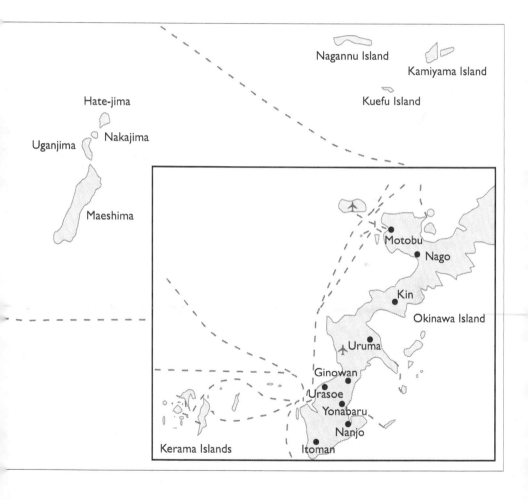

accommodation facilities and an air conditioned Intelligence Room, but also had a large photographic laboratory and a print shop, both of which were under my jurisdiction. In any landing operation, it is extremely valuable to have a large-scale graphic layout of the landing area showing the position of the boats, landing beach, obstructed lanes of approach, and so forth. This seems like a small point, but I believe without question that a skilled graphic presentation can and has saved a great many lives. I had in my section both professional photographers and draftsmen, and between them, they produced remarkable results on paper.

We also received some good, late photographs of our objectives. The photo interpreters poured over them for days searching for clues. There was more evidence of activity, including a great many man-made caves on several of the islands, with tracks of some kind running from them across the beach to the water. Our best guess was that some kind of amphibious craft was housed in the caves, but this guess was not good enough. In early photographs of the Karama Islands, it appeared as if there were easy access to the beaches. On closer observation of the newer pictures, slight breakers were noticed 100 yards off shore in several places, which gave indication of underwater reefs. If they were present, it meant that we could not use ordinary craft LCVPs,[48] but must use amphibious LVTs.[49] It was also important to learn the underwater gradient leading to the beaches. As our system was being developed, one could measure

[48] LCVP - Landing Craft, Vehicle, Personnel, or Higgins boat.

[49] LVT - Landing Vehicle Tracked.

the distance from crest to crest of the waves rolling in from the photographs, and then judge depths. It was by no means perfect, but gave us a rough indication. I mention this as an example of how information can be developed and applied by an Intelligence section to the intricate problem of planning a landing.

Aside from the planning phase, I was charged with the job of keeping up the overall strategic plot of the War of the Pacific. We received dispatches from all active commands in the theater, and on the wall of the Intelligence Room, where it would be plotted constantly. Reports from our submarines and search planes gave almost complete coverage of the Western Pacific, and with occasional intercepts of enemy broadcast, we knew within close range where all his principal Navy units were from day to day. We could also get the Army reports with their front lines each evening which showed our progress in the Philippines. Let me remark that MacArthur's daily reports to the press and the U.S., which we also intercepted, never coincided with the actual situation as transmitted by top secret dispatch. He invariably reported to the press a very expansive picture with at least twice as many Japanese killed as was the case, with half the number of our casualties, and with twice the distance gained. Maybe it was good psychology, but I, for one, can guarantee that it was far from accurate.

Our final exercise before the operation was held on some beaches south of Leyte. There was quite a surf running and several landing boats were swamped on their run to shore; several lives were lost among both the Navy and Army. Preparatory to this exercise, we loaded on board our transport, the

77th Army Division under Major General Bruce.[50] The troops had had considerable experience on the whole, but were not as seasoned as the 37th, which we took to Lingayen.

In the few days preparatory to our departure, we held the usual intensive series of briefings. It is, as I have previously pointed out, an important function of intelligence officers, after all shore communication is cut off, to discuss with all key personnel the exact nature of their assignment and what they may expect to see and encounter. By giving them a graphic and verbal picture of where they are going, they can carry out their assignment with much more intelligence. There were 26 intelligence officers in our whole force. They all reported for several meetings aboard the *McKinley* and were briefed by my intelligence officers and myself, and were given all necessary material—so that they, in turn, could go back to their ships and brief others about the operation. In as much as our operation plan called for the simultaneous assault on six islands, it was of necessity, unusually complex, and required extensive and careful briefing. (Samuel Morrison says, "By good fortune, Hinunangan Bay on Leyte and the Cabugan Islands made possible a remarkably life-like rehearsal of the Kerama landings, which was held on March 13-15. Admiral Kiland, moreover, had an efficient intelligence officer, Lieutenant Commander Ellery Sedgwick, Jr. USNR, whose section got out an illustrated quotation Coxswain's Guide to the Beaches. This the lads studied so carefully during the five-day passage from Leyte that they made no false move.")[51*]

---

[50] Lieutenant General Andrew Davis Bruce commanded the 77th Infantry Division in the Pacific War, active in the campaigns in Guam, Leyte and Ryuku. After the war he served as military governor of Hokkaido and later in 1954 became the third president of the University of Houston.

[51] Samuel Eliot Morrison in his majestic work on the Navy in World War II also cited Sedgwick as the Navy's leading expert on Kamakazes in the Pacific Theater.
* Samuel Morrison Vol XIV pg. 120 (added by E.W.S.)

After these periods, it is always a relief to weigh anchor and be on our way to our objective. We left Leyte about March 22ⁿᵈ, bound for Operation Iceberg. We had four or five days to relax for the most part, and contemplate that Japanese homeland airfields were only 300 miles from our assault area (and, of course, much closer to us on the south). In the course of the journey, we did see some floating Japanese mines in the water. They did no damage and we were later to see literally thousands of these on our travels, but to the best of my knowledge, they never did any material damage.

Because we were the advance echelons, we had a great many reporters on board. It was my job to handle and brief them on the operation. It was not an easy assignment because they always wanted more information than they should be given for security reasons, and they invariably wanted the use of communication facilities that were sorely needed to fight the war. However, they were very decent chaps.

My roommate on the *McKinley* was a British Naval Officer, who was the liaison between our force and the British fleet in the Pacific which consisted of several large cruisers with escorts on the assignment neutralizing enemy bases to the South, particularly Formosa. Our carrier task force (TF-58), under Admiral Spruance,[52] was engaged in neutralizing as many Japanese bases as they could to the north by using hit-and-run tactics.

---

[52] Admiral Raymond H. Spruance commanded the U.S. Naval Forces during many of the most consequential battles in the Pacific. He later became Ambassador for the Philippines.

We arrived off the Karama Islands[53] in the early morning, March 26th. Everything was quiet as the dawn broke with no enemy planes evident and no sign of enemy ashore. Our transports took their positions and unloaded the LTV's amphibious tanks and the troops. There was very little preparatory bombardment because of the absence of enemy shore installations, but our gun boats (LCIs)[54] stood close in to the several beaches to guard the landings. The troops went ashore simultaneously on four islands and then, subsequently, two more. Enemy opposition encountered was only on two of the six and this was quite light. The Japanese retreated into the rugged hills.

Of particular significance was the great number of small motor boats carrying depth charges which were found in caves along the beaches throughout the islands. These were the caves which we had spotted in the photographs and had warned the task force about. In the end, over 400 of these boats were found and destroyed. All were hidden in caves, safe from aerial observation and bombing and with ramps going down into the water. My Japanese Language Officer developed the whole story on these when he went ashore the day following the first landing. In one of the caves, he found a map showing the Japanese plan of action. The enemy never contemplated our going into the seemingly useless islands of Kerama Retto, but expected a major landing ten miles away on the Okinawa beaches on which we did land on April 1st. On the night following the arrival of our transports in the unloading area, some 400-500 of

[53] Off of Okinawa

[54] LCI - Landing Craft Infantry

these suicide boats loaded with TNT would be driven in amongst them and create complete havoc by dropping their charges alongside the ships. It was a clever plan and might have been disastrous had we not moved into Kerama. All the Japanese troops subsequently killed or captured on these islands were boat operators or mechanics and maintenance men. When we learned these facts, the Army proceeded with greatest haste to destroy as many boats as possible, and a close screen of gunboats was thrown around the islands to prevent any sortie. I believe that the record shows that only one ship in the entire force was injured by these suicide boats and not seriously.

When things had become a little quieter, I got a request to send three of the boats to Pearl Harbor for examination. We also kept one or two attached to our ship for use in running errands. They were about 18 feet long, very low in the water, and carried two depth chargers on the fantail, which were set for very shallow depth to explode under the ship's hull. Some were powered with Chevrolet Motors and others with Japanese copies of this engine. They would make about 30 knots.

To return to the operation, all of Kerama Islands were considered secured by the evening of March 26th and the *Mt. McKinley* entered the anchorage area to remain there for over a month. This was probably the worst month I put in during the war, but no one could say it was not interesting. There was never a day without an air alert and on most days, we were at general quarters a large part of the time. The U.S. Navy lost more ships and men (by several times over) during this period than any other in history. This was the responsibility of the "kamikaze," or suicide plane attacks. It was almost the sole form of attack from the air.

Most of the more modern Japanese planes and first line pilots had, by this time, been eliminated, but they had at least 10,000 older planes and never lacked for pilots, most of whom were relatively inexperienced fliers. They would generally leave their home air fields in groups of 10-40 planes, and be guided to the target area by an experienced pilot who often stayed about to observe whether they discharged their duty before he returned to his base. Once in the target area, they would break up and make several uncoordinated attacks on any ship. Most times they appeared to be stupid in the execution of their assignments, selecting unimportant targets, while there were valuable ships close at hand. I have a series of photographs showing one attacking and hitting an LST, when, within a quarter of a mile, there was a carrier. Also, during the time we were at Kerama Retto, almost every other ship of consequence which had been there for any length of time was hit, and yet we in the command ship never were. They sent photo planes over quite frequently, and any proper interpretation of the photos should have shown them our importance.

On the other hand, they fooled us quite frequently by sneaking into the area undetected by our radar screen and picket ships. Sometimes they would come in low over the water from behind the islands which surrounded our anchorage and lift up over them. They would be upon us before there was any time to get to general quarters. We quickly learned that they had assimilated and were employing our own IFF procedure. This was a means of identifying our own incoming planes by a radar transmission which they put up automatically. Several Japanese planes came in using our IFF early in the operation.

Our general defense air attack included a ring of picket ships, generally destroyers, or destroyer escorts about 40-60 miles away from the islands. These were all radar equipped and would warn us of flights coming down from Kyushu. They took a terrible beating and were constantly under attack. The Japanese had an obsession that these had to be knocked out before they could knock out the rest of our ships. For instance, I remember distinctly that one regular Lieutenant Commander reporting to our Admiral, was very proud of having been 22 hours on a picket line without being hit, which was better than par for the course.

Even before we had land-based planes, we maintained our air patrol over the area a large part of the time. These planes, these "CAP" (Combat Air Patrol), were all controlled from our own ship. In a large room below the deck was the control room with its large turnabout screen, on which we marked in crayon the position of all enemy aircraft, as well as reported out by all radar stations. Between 10 and 20 officers were in direct radio connection with our airborne planes, telling them the location of the enemy in relationship to their own positions.

The middle of the day was relatively free from attacks on the whole. One could generally relax. A very large percentage of the planes could be knocked down by our CAP, but almost always got through to attack our shipping. Our anti-aircraft fire brought down more, but even when a kamikaze is hit, he often could run through to the target.

----

*This is the end of Ellery Sedgwick's account. From here on,
the rest of the story is told by quotes from a paper Robert M.
Hamilton wrote from his father, Thomas Hamilton's, memories.
Tom was aide to both Admiral Moon and Admiral Kiland,
and was with Ellery most of the time from before the invasion
of Normandy to the end of the war. They became fast friends.*

We actually had 157 attacks in 58 days, which was the length
of time we were there. Any time an ammunition ship was hit,
any other time in the war, it blew up just like a bomb and cleaned
out the anchorage. One of them had blown up off of Sicily and
sunk every ship around it and another one had blown up in
Seadler Harbor in Manus and sunk every ship around it. This
open roadstead we were in was only a mile-and-a-half long and
a half-mile wide, so we were snuggled up pretty close to these two
ammunition ships. One afternoon a kamikaze came down and
hit one. I was standing on the deck of *McKinley* and it obviously
didn't blow up, or I wouldn't be around dictating this, but it was
an absolute miracle. It just burned like a pile of fireworks for a
couple of hours before it sank and never did explode. There's no
explanation. Nobody has ever come up with an explanation, but
the most miraculous thing is about a half hour after that one was

hit, another Kamikaze came down and hit the other one and they were both burning at the same time and we were expecting, at any second, that either one of them would go up and that would be the end for everybody around there. There's no use being inside the ship, you might as well be up where you can see the fun, so we were standing there watching those things burn.

Kamikaze attacks on Operation Iceberg forces were sporadic before April 6th, probably being restricted to sorties taking off from local airstrips in the Okinawa area. The kamikaze effort, launched against Operation Iceberg forces from the Japanese, was codenamed Operation Ten-Go. On April 6th, Ten-Go got going.

The word "kamikaze" has entered the language. It is the simplest of guided missiles, an airplane with a suicide pilot. Born of desperation, they proved terribly and cruelly effective. They were accurate, and even without the bomb or torpedo each customarily carried, the projectile was large enough to do considerable damage to topside surfaces and personnel, had sufficient kinetic energy to penetrate interior structures (particularly since the engine served as a crude 'penetrator), and worst of all, spewed flaming aviation gas indiscriminately. A disproportionately large number of kamikaze casualties were burn victims, which is the hardest kind of casualty to care for.

At the battle of Okinawa, kamikazes were opposed by a defense of nested layers. The first, and most effective layer was CAP (Combat Air Patrol) projected over the area by carriers assigned for that purpose. Navy fighters would intercept kamikazes as far from their targets as possible. The CAP were guided by the picket screen. These were destroyer-type ships stationed at strategic points around the area perimeter, whose radar would locate incoming attackers, and whose air controllers would vector CAP fighters to their targets. Kamikazes which broke through to the ships were engaged at medium range by the next layer, five-inch guns on destroyers and larger screen vessels. By 1945, five-inch anti-aircraft shells were equipped with proximity fuses which greatly increased their effectiveness. At short range, attackers were engaged by the innermost layer—40mm and 20mm anti-aircraft guns—usually in multiple-mount "gun tubs." These rapidly firing weapons could put up a withering curtain of fire. Each of these layers was effective, and together they defeated a lot of kamikazes.

The Japanese responded by sending many kamikazes at once in an attempt to saturate the defenses. This often worked, as did sending them at dawn and dusk when gunnery was less efficient. They also came at night. They sank a lot of ships, damaged many more, and caused grave numbers of casualties.

Ellery Sedgwick, who was by this time the Chief Intelligence Officer (on Kiland's staff), decided that he ought to go out to reach one of the ships that had been under kamikaze attack and had survived. Of course, that usually meant that they were hit, but if they didn't sink and they got back to anchorage, he'd go over to them and see what he could find out about the kamikaze attacks. *Did they come in out of the sun? Did they come in low over the horizon? What time of day?* He recorded all he could find out about them that might be useful to these poor guys that were coming up there and going out. He set up a kind of doctrine he had typed up, and I had it reproduced for him. It was simply to tell the incoming skippers what we knew about kamikazes and, of course, we knew more about them than anybody in the world because we'd had all these attacks and were still there.

Sedgwick put together this dope and we gave it to the skippers of the new division of destroyers as they came in. Well, each thing that leaves a flag office, or any other Navy command, has to have a date-time-group on it. Every Navy yeoman is indoctrinated with that into the marrow of his bones, otherwise there is no way to identify what goes out unless you have the thing to read. So each copy of Sedgwick's document got a date-time-group ID when it was given to a new skipper. They thought it was great to have and, unknown to us, they sent it back upstream to their squadron commander and then he sent it further up, and so we got a request for more copies from the Commanders of destroyers in the Pacific Fleet. When the Admiral saw this, he blew his lid and wanted to know what it was, and I told him. He sent for Sedgwick. He lined us up against the bulkhead at attention and announced that Sedgwick was not the senior officer around there, that Admiral Turner[55] was, and that he was not authorized to issue any doctrine. He said we had no authority to do anything like this, and if we did anything like it again, he was going to send us both to Portsmouth Naval Prison. He ordered us to destroy all the copies of this thing. Well, we didn't do that. We hid a couple, so we'd have them, I don't know exactly what our plans were, but we did that. In a few more days another division of destroyers came up and a Commander of a squadron of destroyers came in and made such a pitch about how important it was that he have this. Sedgwick joined in with him and persuaded me

---

[55] Admiral Kelly Turner commanded the Amphibian Force in the Pacific. He created the Underwater Demolition Teams that were a precursor to the Navy Seals.

to make up another bunch of them, but we swore him to secrecy. We said, "You can give them to your ship captains if that's what you want them for, but don't let anybody else know about it." And he promised... Things went along quietly for a few days, and then *zingo*, we got a signal from Admiral Nimitz, Commander-in-Chief of the Pacific, wanting some copies of this thing, and low-and-behold, it has a different date-time-group on it, so the Admiral almost struck us. I thought he was going to hit us physically, but he didn't, he just swore at us and promised us Portsmouth again. So we went out and we had another huddle, and we said, "Look, we've got to knock this off. This old guy means it." So we agreed no more, no more. Well, one night it was cold and rainy—this was early spring in Okinawa—and the wind was blowing. A messenger got me out of my sack about midnight, and I went down to the flag office. Here was a Navy Commander, and he looked like he'd been swimming in his uniform. He was cold, shaking, and dripping, and it turned out that he was the commander of a division of destroyers that had just been ordered in. He was going up on Picket Station #1. He had come across the open roadstead in an open boat in the rain and wind because he said that he had talked to the skippers of the destroyers that had come back from Okinawa. They had simply told him that he couldn't take his destroyers in there without getting the latest copy of the doctrine we had because it was bad enough anyhow, but it was suicide without it. Well, I couldn't stand it, so I rousted out some yeomen. Sedgwick had updated his document, and I got the updated copy, and I got these yeomen, and I swore them to secrecy. I swore them to use the same old date-time-group and we made a bunch and gave them to him. Everything was fine, and then low and behold, in about four days we got a signal from, this time, the Chief of Naval Operations, Admiral King. The watch had been changed (while the copies were being prepared) and a new yeoman had come in, and it had a new date-time-group on it. Well, I didn't know whether the Admiral was going to die of a stroke or a heart attack or shoot both of us, but it was a memorable scene. Fortunately, we got ordered away before it happened again, and they ran out of kamikazes.

To put this *contretemps* into perspective, the ordeal of the picket destroyers at Okinawa was horrible. Reading Morrison on Okinawa is to encounter page after page of descriptions of kamikaze attacks and hits, mostly all upon screen destroyers. On page 234 of Volume XIV appears a diagram, *Air Attacks on U.S.S. Laffey, 16 April 1945*. In appalling simplicity, it shows the tracks of twenty-two separate aircraft which attacked during an 80-minute period. Eighteen were shot down (a remarkable performance for a single ship of any type); six got through and struck the ship. This is the kind of carnage that Sedgwick (and Hamilton) were trying to stop. Rear Admiral Kiland was correct, it was not his place to issue doctrine; Vice Admiral Turner had ordered the destroyers to picket duty, so it was his responsibility to promulgate anti-kamikaze doctrine. But, he wasn't doing anything, and something badly needed to be done—ships were sinking and men were dying.

The following passage gives some small insight into Vice Admiral Turner's character, and goes some way toward explaining why Rear Admiral Kiland may have been reluctant to issue doctrine.

The other thing that I remember about Okinawa was that we were there so long that we ran into typhoon season. We didn't actually have a typhoon while we were there, but they were about three weeks overdue, and we should have had two or three of them. That so, we had to set-up a plan to evacuate the place if a typhoon came along because we were responsible for all those ammunition ships, gasoline tankers, fuel tankers, all the crippled ships, all the repair tenders, and whatever we had in there. We had to get them out where they'd have a chance to get to the open sea, rather than being dead ducks in the roadstead. Admiral Turner should have done this, but he wouldn't do it for some reason known only to him. So the Chief of Staff (Capt. Tomkins) persuaded Admiral Kiland that we ought to do it, and he prepared an evacuation plan in the event of a typhoon. The Admiral then sent the Chief of Staff over to Admiral Turner, who was, of course, our boss, and who was lying off Buckner Bay on his flagship to get permission to send this thing out and around. Well, for some reason, I guess the Chief of Staff felt lonesome, and he knew something of Admiral Turner, so he asked me if I'd like to go with him. Actually, he said, "Come on Hamilton, let's go." (Which is a command, but he was smiling; I could have gotten permission to stay. Anyhow, I wanted to go with him.) We went over and I stood outside the cabin while he went in to see the Admiral. Now Turner was usually gassed by about 10 a.m. in the morning, and he was an irascible old SOB anyway, but he finally got through his head what Tomkins had and he said, "If I want a typhoon procedure put out, I'll put it out. It's not your place to issue doctrine. Now I will give you 30 seconds to get off of my flagship, or I'll have you thrown off. Dismissed." Capt. Tomkins came out, and we got off the flaship in the allotted 30 seconds.

I always assumed that Turner's (and hence Kiland's) disinclination to issue anti-kamikaze doctrine was simple incompetence (although in many ways Admiral Turner was a very able commander), until I came upon a disturbing reference while researching this paper. Admiral Nimitz, Admiral Halsey and several thousand other sailors were worried about this Kamikaze Corps. Its pilots made no return trips, but almost one in every four found a target and did some damage, and one in thirty-three sank a ship. Experts were set to work on the problem, and a tight censorship cloaked the whole dismal project. Officers and men returning to the continents of Australia and North America were warned not to mention the kamikazes, and mail was carefully scrutinized for any hint of them lest the enemy learn how much damage he was doing. From this point of view, secrecy was effective; the Japanese air forces claimed a ship to every pilot expended, but never really knew the score. Not until April 1945, during the Okinawa campaign, when it was impossible to suppress the news any longer, did the Pentagon break one of the greatest news stories of the war. It so happened that the kamikaze story was revealed the same day (the 12th) that the death of President Roosevelt shook the Allied public; consequently, it received comparatively little attention.

Thus, as the war against the Japanese drew to its close, Okinawa became a giant air and naval base. For it, we paid a heavy price. Thirty-two naval ships and craft had been sunk, mostly by kamikaze attack, and 368 ships and craft had been damaged. The Fleet lost 763 aircraft. Over 4,900 sailors were killed or went missing-in-action, and an additional 4,824 were wounded. This was by far the heaviest loss incurred in any naval campaign in the war. These losses do not include Army casualties afloat and ashore: 7,613 killed/missing; 31,807 wounded; and 26,000 non-battle casualties.

On August 6, 1945, a B-29 bomber dropped an atomic bomb on Hiroshima, and on August 9th, a second bomb was dropped on Nagasaki. The war was quickly over and the intelligence group, which was already helping plan the invasion of Japan, was dismantled. Ellery Sedgwick, being the head of the group, was the last to leave (except for M. Parrish, who was a bachelor). He returned home on about December 1, 1945.